Editorial

This issue has been hugely delayed by many things: two major computer break-downs, leading to months of frustration; running the show mostly solo when a staff of at least three is needed; personal matters – all leading to lost motivation, morale, stamina (I could go on …) But from somewhere I found at last the 'whatever' to finish this. I apologise profusely to subscribers, readers and others involved – and especially to contributors who have waited, understanding and patient, for it to appear – with 176 pages instead of 144! A small bonus! I hope this will be a sign of things to come – a larger magazine appearing perhaps twice yearly, to make up the same annual number of pages.

Angus first: he was a major force for good in the land, and his compulsion to stick his thumb into every important cultural pie going helped bring about remarkable progress in many spheres. But there was a personal cost, for which in later years he paid in full. He couldn't resist a call to arms in a good cause, pooh-poohed personal welfare and sallied on regardless. Latterly, people had to combine to rescue him ("Angus's dream team" as Bill Dunlop christened us), helping him out of his domicile in Spittal Street. A major operator in this was accountant Eric Wishart as I'm sure every member of said dream team would be happy to recognise. It was among Angus's unpaid bills that Eric found the unpublished poems included here. The memoirs and reflections *not* 'tributes'! from friends and colleagues in this issue do not sidestep 'the darker side' of Angus, yet all confirm his tireless commitment to so many of the 'right things' that leave us, as a nation, as a world, greatly – miraculously enriched. George Gunn suggests that Scotland ate Angus Calder – and I think that insightful and true – in many ways we failed him in not paying the bill for the meal or leaving an encouraging tip. Finally, I commend you to the anthology *For Angus*, produced by Richard Burns and Gideon Calder (see leaflet).

There is incredible bounty and variety in the work assembled here, which I hope you will enjoy. I'm especially delighted to include here the fine poetry of Gerry Stewart, a previous assistant, who gave so much to *Chapman* for nearly five years – and first-rate work from Colin Donati, Eleanor Livingstone, Rob MacKenzie, Alan Riach and Gerda Stevenson, all of whom are making serious contributions in diverse cultural fields. Regular publication of *Chapman* will resume after what has been a very nasty 'sabbatical'. We *will* need help, especially in these 'difficult times' in which so many small presses and enterprises such as ours are going to the wall, or struggling to avoid it (Salt, Two Ravens, Dedalus – even Chambers!…). I am acutely conscious of and grateful for the great community of good people and good will that has built up around the magazine over many years and take especial heart from the recent translation of Janet Paisley's *Alien Crop* into Ukrainian which reminds me that the effort's more than worth it. I hope I can count on your continuing support!

Graham Fulton

Tone Deaf, Auschwitz, Poland

At gas chamber 2 at Birkenau
a mobile phone goes off
as we stand in nauseous awe
of SS butchers   rotten things
that men have done

It makes
a cock-a-doodle-doo sound   pops
our mood with callous style
a wake up call for those
who can't

Genocide rails recede
to the gate
Orthodox Jews say prayers
in the trees

The phoneman answers
and tells the caller
exactly where he is   then laughs

Dark Age Rage

In a gallery hung with Renaissance art
an iPodded boy in a *Road Hog* shirt
is emptily dragging his thumbnail across
some unprotected enlightened paint.

Tintoretto's *Ordeal of Tuccia* –
made it this far for hundreds of years
but met its match in a Glasgow twat.
You can hear the endangered figures scream.

Somehow, it wouldn't seem so bad
if he knew he was doing something wrong.
He's blank, his eyes are permafrost.
His nuclear mother and father, blank.

It's somewhere to go before The Mall.
They're probably taking him downstairs to prod
the dead stuffed elephant, Great Auk egg.
He'd loved to have pulled the trigger himself.

Chariots of Rage

On the beach where
        Ian Charleson splashed –
    Vangelis and Liddell,
              arms, legs,
slowed to give
  an illusion
      of strength
                  Royal   Ancient
          phantoms of sand,
    swept from dunes by mythic winds,
battering all that's left in their path:
golfballs, gulls,
      woman, her dog,
a dot, sun,   a mile long arc,
Antarctic flow,   St. Andrews in March
is not for the fragile of heart,
        the gods

uncompromising primordial rush,
wild,   perpetually
     moving walkway,
   meeting the North Sea tide head on,
equal, pure,   Olympus in Fife,
long dead actor,   heroes in shorts,
making the breakers bend and fizz,
nature surf
upon itself.

The Last King of Glasgow (13 September, 2006)

A musty Mesozoic display
decades beyond its dump-by-date
Ex-T Rex! Lizard King!
The *Kelvingrove One*
         is now extinct

He reckoned he had a job for life
ruling the *Creatures From the Past*
They've bumped him off
         wheeled him out
He's gone to the tar pit
in the sky

It's just as well   the CGI kids
would laugh and point
                          piss their pants
when they saw
his wobbly Sixties teeth
spindly arms   bandy legs
a softy from a cut-and-paste age

Farewell
          my mis-proportioned friend
who ROARED above me
                    helped me dream
Museum piece! Magnificent chump!

We couldn't keep up with HD bones
                    21st Century spoon-fed thrills
There's no room left
for worlds of our own

Dry Bones, Peru

1
Nazca exhibit, pots and freaks.
It's just two sol for a camera pass,
I'll get a shot of a mummified child.

Alien-warped, butter bean head,
viced with cords and stretched by a priest
at birth, abused, spaceman chic.

The Spanish caption requires no sense.
A fashion victim, kneeling, bowed,
voyeured, de-organed. Steak-brown flesh.

Von Daniken girl, a skull so fine
would cave with the season's softest rain.
I feed like a leech, can't help myself.

A precious pain I collect on film,
carefully angle the flash, make sure
my shame is reflected back on the glass.

2
Inside the church of San Francisco
visitors peer down into a well
to see the famous wheel of bones.

Skulls at the hub, femurs for spokes.
Who can say which skull belongs
to what big thigh? A catacomb club.

Concentric circles, cranial art.
Litter and coins dropped over the rim
vanish,
       tidily,
            find their place.

Outside in the light, blue-smocked nurses
raise their placards, chain their arms,
sing some songs for a fairer wage.

They move in shapes inside of shapes.
The rings of Lima, turn through space,
turn to God, get carried away.

Who can say which soul belongs
to what big smile? They're disappeared.

3
The air's not there.
                I'm pacing my breath
on altitude Lake, the wind is a slap.

I hold a bone I found on the beach
and re-enact the Dawn of Man
from Stanley Kubrick's 2001.
I batter the bone against a stone
and launch it into the Darwinist sky.

Inca kids in mix
          and match strips
play football beside a small white church.
The idols here are leather and round.
The children keep their feet on the ground.

The ball is ballooned towards the sun.
A bone-shaped spaceship drops on my head.

Unlike the ball
         which does not stop
it's learned the law which makes us fall.

Suicide Dogs of Ecclefechan
Rob McClure Smith

Paranormal investigators and an animal communicator have been called in by the Dumfries police to investigate the reason dogs have been killing themselves by leaping off the old Grassic Bridge. The bridge, which straddles the Fechan burn outside historic Grassic House, was in the news in March last year after five dogs plunged 40 feet to their deaths within a six month period. No explanation has yet been found for the behaviour, which has continued to baffle local residents and animal experts. (*Ecclefechan Advertiser*, 9/20/05)

My mother's father was an odd duck. I'm not denying it. The old chap was something of a scholar, an antiquarian, a man of peculiar tenets. He may have been a minor dabbler in the dark arts in his younger days. That's magic with a K, if you will. He was ever a seeker. Absolutely in his latter years he had turned a trifle batty. As will we all, I might add. Alzheimer's we surmised. Frankly, it was a relief to the family when he passed on. Near the end he had taken to believing he was a shuttlecock or some such thing, always bothering people to play badminton with him. And I mean *with* him. But there was never the slightest suggestion of witchcraft, or that the house and its environs were haunted. I've heard the rumours of strange occult rites since I was a child, of dim black masses by the old cairn. Poppycock. My grandfather was a Peer of the Realm for heaven's sake. He voted against the foxhunting ban, paid his taxes, was a longtime supporter of Queen of the South F C. He wore his underwear like the next man. (Earl Douglass of Grassic, Interview, 10/6/04)

I felt lots of wee children scrabbling at my legs as I walked across and I felt myself distinctly being drawn across to the right-hand side. Yes, I was definitely pulled. I also felt very sick and uncomfortable at certain stanchions and sometimes it was as if my feet were sinking in the bridge, like it was a sticky wet tar or a smooth liquid jelly maybe. (John from Glasgow, SAPI team member, ectoplasmic #3)

Ah wis jist ower yonder by the willow break when ah see Roy take aff and afore ah know it he's up there oan the bridge, hangin ower. Ah wis well aware o the history o thaim suicide dogs so ah'm up there lickety-split an ah grab hold o that mutt right quick afore he does fur himself tae. Cowerin like a leaf in a windstorm that yin wis. Growlin as well. Scared shitless. (Pardon mah French, mon sewer). Me an mah dug baith actually. (Alan Gordon, former Grassic estate ghillie, Interview, 17/6/04)

Then once I saw myself that Nellie leaning flat against the wall of the bridge with nothing on but her stockings and the pearls cooling her throat like that. You know how I like it, she says me, like that, and hurrying her mouth into mine, other girls swirls with roulette eyes and voices like a perfume slide over bricks, like that. Black dripping wires chasing crows. Long times go there was a beast lives there. (Interview Transcript file 17, Patient MS, 15/6/94)

Many Native American and aboriginal peoples communicated with animals quite naturally. This skill has been lost this millennium and now requires substantial cultivation and educative training. If we want to recommunicate with other species, we need to work on deconstructing our messages down into concrete images, rather than language-based artifacts. When one is comfortable in the image interflow, in my own experience, conversations with animals can cover a wide array of interesting subjects. Interchange prompts might range from "How are you doing today?" to "What do you feel about euthanasia?" or from "Who do you think will win the Premier League this year?" to "What do you think of my new boyfriend?" Horses in particular have decided opinions about most everything, especially the Blair Government. (Elle Bree Bechtold, 'Hello, Mrs Doolittle', *Lifestyles Profile*, Dumfries Register Mail)

I have never in all my life heard of a dog committing suicide. And I don't think for one minute some animal goes strolling along the bridge and suddenly think to itself "Ach, I can't go on. I can't take it any more". And then goes and jumps to its death. I mean it's just too ludicrous for words. If you ask me, there's a rational explanation for the suicide dog phenomenon, likely more than one. I know for definite the last thing our local constabulary needed to do was import some halfwit teuchter animal-whisperer. (Millie Davies, canine behaviourist, interview, 27/9/05)

The bridge lies in the grounds of Grassic House, an A-listed baronial building nestling in the shadow of Burnswark hill. This bridge was the scene of a notorious tragedy in 1994 when Michael Stallard, a local secondary teacher, threw his two-week-old daughter from the parapet to her death believing her to be the Antichrist. Stallard was found incompetent to stand trial and institutionalised. (*Ecclefechan Advertister*, 20/9/05)

I absolutely had a sense of children being there and a strong negative feeling coming at me from the far end of the bridge. I also sensed the presence of a man who was possibly a minister, or maybe a motor mechanic. The man kept saying he didn't understand evolution. He said, "I can't assimilate what I know as a Christian with Darwin." And then he said something about a carburettor as well, kept on about how come the plug line was clogged with oil. He seemed really upset about it. (Mishka from Birmingham, SAPI team member, ectoplasmic #7)

I'm a sceptic. No question. Colour me dubious. But five dogs have expired after jumping from that selfsame spot. So I think owners should at least best keep their animals on a leash when crossing. Better safe than sorry. I'm thinking it might be to do with the static electricity generated by the water current there, or something of that nature. You know, I just read in the *The Herald* last month that this here part of the borders is one of the most depressing places to live in the United Kingdom. But I assumed that meant for humans, not dogs. (Doreen Cameron, Scottish Society for the Prevention of Cruelty to Animals, Interview, 22/8/05)

Obviously a person can analyse why these dogs jumped till the cows come home. Mind you, when the cows do come home they'd like as not be jumping in the Fechan too the way things are going. I have no idea why they do it. Nor did my erstwhile permanently-soused ghillie. The drunkard's mutt got in on the act too latterly. I've heard all the explanations, the canine depression and the poltergeists and so on and so forth. If I had a theory it would be this: Superman's dog. You'll recall how Clark Kent's dog can fly. I once saw a TV programme about him. I believe his name is Krypto. Krypto the Superdog. My recollection is this individual has a little doggy cape like his master's which flaps out behind his tail when he rockets round the stratosphere. It's blue. Ergo: if these so-called suicide dogs saw this chap Krypto swooshing around on the idiot box, they might suppose they could be airborne too. Your average dog is very impressionable. Have you seen the collies with the sheep? Putting them in pens, I mean. Remarkable. Respond to whistling they do. Much like loose women. Would you believe that Thomas Carlyle used to sit in that very chair you're in now? Yes, the Bard of Ecclefechan himself once parked his arse on that selfsame cushion. Your buttocks would be immersed in history there, young fellow. But I wouldn't let the old canines near a plasma television. Bound to give the blighters ideas. (Earl Douglass)

The Scottish Association for Paranormal Inquiry (SAPI) visited the site last spring and documented sensing "ghostly ministers, a mysterious Victorian woman and grasping children". In a recently-published report on her 10-strong team's findings, team leader Janet Little observed: "There were numerous correlations in what our people felt. Three felt anxious, sad, depressed and disorientated and four others sensed very negative feelings. There were definitely themes of upset children: several of the team mentioned a Victorian woman in a grey shawl crouching at the end of the bridge." Little emphasised that none of the psychic investigators had prior knowledge about the bridge and the only information she had given them was about the dogs. Little is herself an expert on the paranormal valence of bridges. (*Ecclefechan Advertiser*)

Ah huv a multiplicity o theories, Jim. Bit the best wid be there's a trace o whisky in the watter. Aye, the distillery is up yonder an the process is bound tae git the stuff in the burn. Way ah look at it, the dugs can sense the yeast an barley. Same way they hear high pitch sounds we cannae. It attracts them. Ah tell ye, mony's the time ah've found Roy wi a big tongue in mah shot glass. No that he's goat a problem. Spite of whit yon Bechtold wumman says. Bit considur this: whit if the dugs intended tae droon theyselves in whisky. Wid that be suicide, eh? Ah mean, whit a way tae go! Ah'd be intae that masel. (Gordon)

Grassic House was built in 1763 by the Marquis of Grassic and renovated in 1947 by James Douglass, grandfather of the current Earl. The latter had the words 'Fear God and keep His commandments well' carved into its walls alongside a frieze of images of the Egyptian deity Horus. Local historians describe the house today as an odd architectural mishmash where inscriptions and etchings of angels and bizarre gargoyles keep strange company. (Alan Stuart, *Baronial Homes of Scotland*, p 67)

My sense was of a kind of workman in blue overalls and an old checked cloth bunnet. He was crying. I imagine he'd been working on the bridge and fallen to his death and now was down in the gully calling the dogs to join him. Right enough, why this person would want a dog is anybody's guess. Perhaps he had a thing for dogs when he was alive? Lots of working men kept greyhounds back in the 40s. There was a track hereabouts, I'm told. (Elaine, Aberdeen, SAPI team member, ectoplasm #10)

I incorporate Reiki Healing Touch, Tellington T-Touch, Flower Essence Therapy and other salve-healing methods as to support well-being for animals and more satisfying relationships with their people friends. What I intend to do is to facilitate the conversation between the police and the traumatized animal thus enabling the parties mutually to learn more about each other's needs and desires. You see a dog is a window – helps see the person from the inside out. And vice-versa. (Bechtold)

Bridges are such magical places. Iris, the messenger Goddess, is a bridge. In Christianity, Pope means 'builder of bridges', from the Latin word 'pontifex'. The bridge to Paradise in Islam, which is a single thin hair sharp as a razor, swings over Hell. So Christians and Moslems both have their bridges! The Buddha is also said to be the bridge by which you cross the intersection of the Six Paths. (Janet Little, Interview, 30/9/05)

The house. Covering up the secret of the lies, hiding in cover, a clover, an underclover detective from Bakes-Ville, where white lies to cover up the black lies is a grey shawl girl. To shut my mouth no nothing tooth picks. A man with plaid pants and one two glow yellow dog eyes in the dark. Burns. Hide behind a clown's mask and pretend to be real. Just that. The man in the box is telling me to be quiet, always quiet. Shhh. There's something wrong with this channel. (Transcript file MS, 15/6/94)

Between you an me yon Earl is nutty as a fruitcake. Jist like the rest o the family. It's true whit they say: if yir poor yir mad, if yir rich yir jist eccentric. That Graham shower wid be eccentric tae beat the band an it's a right loony o the furst watter bides up there noo. Ah mind we hud a problem wi the foxes. Breedin like rabbits wis they foxes, if ye see whit ah mean. This wid be aboot three weeks afore ah wis fired. They wee bampots wis intae everythin. So ah ask the man if he reckons industrial poison is the answer fur Reynard an he started oan aboot how twelve fit tall lizards wur in charge o the government an how this wisnae a guid situashun. Ah wid tend tae agree, bit that didnae help us any wi the fox scenario. Ah says, "Ur Tony Blair an Gordon Brown kind o geckos then, sir?" He looks at me like ah'm the wan is nuts an shakes his heid. "Tortoises?" ah ask. "Not *that* government," he says, aw crabbit. "Not the *human* government, man." Whitever. Ah felt quite damn stupid, tell ye the truth. (Gordon)

The 14th Earl was a Minor Adept of the Hermetic Order of the Golden Dawn and close friend of William Butler Yeats and the Bhikkhu Ananda Metteyya. Later, he would re-affiliate with Aleister Crowley's OTO, prior to the group's schism of the 1930s. As a British officer in Egypt in 1945 the Earl claimed to channel a "praeterhuman intelligence" named Sekehmet-ra-Wep-wawe in the lavatory of a Cairo brothel. On his return, among other modifications, he ordered the stele of Ankh-af-na-khonsu installed in the fireplace of Grassic House. His daughter, and the mother of the current laird, Nuit Ma Ahathoor Hecate Sappho Jezebel Lilith Graham, was born in London in 1925. (Stuart, *Baronial Homes of Scotland*)

Let me put it to you like this: every man and woman who reaches the upper levels of spiritual and intellectual development feels the presence of some Higher Intelligence. Socrates called it his daemon. The *plebes* call it gods or angels. Maybe it's just another part of our brain, a part we usually don't use, who knows? I suspect I only use a part of my brain. But it's evident to anyone who considers the question seriously that the Higher Intelligences are embedded in our language and numbers, and that all that exists is information and coding. Of course, it's crucial to the powers-that-be we continue to imagine we have bodies and live in space-time dimensions and all that palaver. (Earl of Douglass)

For example, I talked to this one architect chap and he took one look at the design of the trusses and said that the bridge would likely affect an optical illusion for a small animal crossing it. See, at a dog's level it looks like there's a wall on either side so they're not even aware that they're on a bridge but at the same time they can also still hear what's going on around them, the rush of water on the rocks below and so on, and might become too curious. So they hop up there on the railing to take a gander and if it's slippery with wet spray they're over the edge swift before they realise the danger. So in this case I'd be tempted to claim that curiosity killed the dog. A cat likely wouldn't be that stupid in the first place. (Davies)

From my sessions with the animal so far I have received intuitive information in clairsentience, clairaudience and claircognisance. On occasion said information transmigrated through all three modalities at once. Roy is a quick talker and very intellectual. I gather that he was extraordinarily depressed that he hadn't been for a walk earlier that evening. Roy harbors a great many resentments, extending from a difficult puppy-hood, but I have tasked him to work through these emotional blockages now in a productive and proactive manner. Strategies will be applied. Categorically though, there was nothing remotely supernatural involved in the bridge incident. Also, Roy was a tad upset still about a rubber ball he'd been chewing and misplaced. (Bechtold)

A waterwheel of folding fractions, windswills over springs of freshwater. Sadness toppled with candycoat and sugarbears. Big starbirds flocking silver beads stencil heads with peppermint mouths sugary still and with a turn of a cheek he sneaks into a cheat. Other things. Faces swarm a broken mirror I hide in my pocket. You can't know to say it one. The boxes shift, ajar, afar, a poppy pamphlet slops out a file and a little girl is there. Piles of smiles, I say hello. My own little one. Hello, little my girl. (Transcript file MS, 6/15/94)

I'll tell you what I think. I'll tell you. There's war in Heaven. Absolutely. The Higher Intelligences, whoever they are, aren't all playing on the same team. No. Some of them try to encourage our evolution to the higher altitudes, and others want us stuck just where we are. It's imperative that we work with the nonhuman intelligences that want to accelerate human evolution. But it's hard. The *gnosis* is stymied by the Freemasons. Every single time the energy is raised and large-scale group illuminations are occurring, the local branch of the Inquisition up and kills it dead. It happened with Mesmer's animal magnetism, with Reichenbach's *od*, with Gurnitsch's mitogenic ray, with Reich's orgone energy. Why? They take your thoughts with wires. That's why. Thank you, Agnes. You can leave the tray there. Would you be wanting crumpets with your tea now? A meringue? Just a smidgeon maybe? (Earl Douglass)

Then in the Celtic sagas of the Mabinogi, King Bran stretches himself over Shannon and his entire army rides over him. Not to mention how Bifrost in Nordic mythology extends from Midgard to Asgard. And that's just the religions and mythologies. Don't even get me started on folktales like 'Billy Goats Gruff'! I know tons and tons about bridges. I know a lot more about bridges than anything else practically. (Little)

"Woof, woof, woof, woooo ..." (Remus, as reported by owner Agnes McFadden, 17/3/04)

Ah tell ye this, Jim. If ah wis surrounded by half the nutjobs that hang oot aroon this toon, an ah wis a dug masel, ah'd huv jumped a while back. In fact, the mair whackos turn up in these parts the mair ah'm startin tae seriously considur it. Them dugs jist couldnae take it. An ye know whit, Jim? Ah cannae say ah fuckin blame them. (Gordon)

Eleanor Livingstone

Enough Rope

You could not scissor your legs
around the rope, feel the scratch
of its length, or the bunch of the knot
between your thighs while standing
on the cliff edge, the rope was too short,
the knot too high; you had to launch yourself
into space, jump
                    from the jutting shelf of rock

which on wet mornings bled red clay on socks
and shorts; you had to leap into the ravine
above large boulders and the rush of the burn
ten feet below, with only inches of rope
grasped in your fists, one tight
above the other;

                    you had to go for it,
confident you'd find the rope, the knot,
that perfect moment of connection
out there in mid air above the ravine;

you had to go for it, again and again,
throw your heart off that cliff, your words
to the wind for the free-fall buzz of it,
the scissor-knot of it, the rope burn,
the high flying once in a lifetime chance
to go for it. Or let it go.

August Again

the dandelion clock
will be gone in a moment

and the child who holds it
in one plump hand
exact on a milky stem
gone too before this century is out

the grassy hill she walks across

following after her

The Scottish Chip

Remnants of a lost lunch lie scattered
around Robert Fergusson's feet and mine
where a bird grabs at them in turn, tossing them
like cabers. This grey-feathered athlete
is a tourist attraction for Italian school parties
and middle-aged Irish women who pause
for photo opportunities beside me and the poet
Get your hands out of his pockets, Eileen!
en route for Holyrood. The bird carries on
regardless, eye to the main chance, seeing off
other pigeons who venture too close. Throwing
his weight around, he stabs and tosses away.
Chips fly around Fergusson's head, and mine.
Sassy, confident, effective beaked, he hurls
the dwindling stock: this pigeon has no chip
on his shoulder; though soon Fergusson and I do.

Textual Analysis

Once upon a time
when you were three or four, for weeks,
perhaps because of the dog's face
on the cover, you insisted on falling asleep
with a library copy of *Woof!* in your arms.
You were too young to understand the text
or even have it read to you, but every morning
I'd find it snuggled warm under the covers.

Before *Woof!*, and after, there had been
and would be other books which,
if laid dog-eared end to end
could have reached our local library
and back again; board books, all the bears
big and brown and Bramwell, the bears
who couldn't sleep, bears in pyjamas
or Wellington boots; Heidi, the Topsy
who never grew up, and Tim, even
the odd middle-aged *Famous Five*
or *Castle of Adventure*
fallen out of an earlier childhood;
and we spelled out the words together.

You still fall asleep with a book
on your chest, but now making your bed
in the morning, I find, tangled in the covers
The Coming of The Third Reich,
or *A Streetcar Named Desire;*
and the words you don't understand
are 'autarchy' and 'monocausal',
beyond the scope of my dictionary:
they have to be looked up on-line.

The boy who turned into a dog
has run off into the night, and the girl
who hugged that book to sleep
is off on her own adventure.

The Day the Music ...
April 1982

Down on my knees
cleaning the skirting boards,
I'm wringing out a damp rag
in a basin of dirty water,
listening to the radio
      when I hear the news.

Born after Korea and Suez,
we grew to adulthood believing that war
was fought on the pages of history books,
in old black and white films on Sunday afternoons
or elsewhere, someone else's problem
on the TV news each night;
      even Ireland
was not quite here, not quite
war, not quite ours.

When the radio announces we are 'at war',
I'm down on my knees staring at the wall
above the now clean skirting board,
the dirty rag in my hands
drowned in the basin beside me,
the chill of the cooled water
creeping up my arms: I'm on my knees
but already it's too late to pray.

Alastair Marshall

The One Sun/Chimera Shimmerer

I took an intuitive leap
into the deep
and the deep said, We are one
reflected by the sun.

And the sun said, I think,
on reflection, you are right.

And I said, That's right enough,
I reckon. We are one. Quite possibly
we are the sun *and* its reflection.

And the reflection said, Huh, what a chimera,
shows how much you know.

And the consequence was ...
we squabbled, the intuitive leap
leapt back to its source,
and the poem came to an abrupt.

a working title

all writing is an experiment
some experiments work
this writing is an experiment
that's very lazy

The Nihilist's Prayer

Our Zero, which art in all,
sallowed be thy name. Thy noughtness come.
Thy torpor be done, on earth
as it is in dead space.
Give us this day our daily dead
and ignore our trespasses
as we ignore those we trespass against.
And lead us not into sensation
but deliver us a weevil,
for thine is the noughtness,
the dour and the hoary,
for ever and ever, Amen.

Résumé

I won't pull the trigger
(of a shotgun with my toe).
I won't start slashing
(my wrists with a razor).
I won't drown myself
(in a river/sea/lake/pool/pond).
I won't jump off a building or bridge
(one that's sufficiently high).
I won't throw myself away
(in front of a speeding express train).
I won't swallow pills
(to excess, the door locked).
I won't dispose of my head
(in a gas oven).
I won't ingest poison
(weedkiller or something better).
I won't hang myself
(with a belt/sheet/rope).

Not that I've given much thought
to killing myself.

Sum Ergo Cogito

I think
that if I didn't think,
I'd be happy.

I've a good mind
(I'm in two minds
about that) to commit

mental suicide,
but is my mind worth
killing? (I think not.)

I feel
that happiness is
a state (totalitarian

of course) of mind
over matter like
the body or the brain.

My Favourite Things
Cynthia Rogerson

All day, I sit. I do not have to use my hands, my legs, my mind, or even my eyes, which I frequently close. I fall into a dream, without falling off my chair. I can sleep with my eyes open. I've no idea what I look like, but I assume I appear quite normal. No drool. Every month when I notice my pay has gone into my bank account, I breathe two sighs – one of relief and one of astonishment. How do I get away with this?

Alone? No, not alone – anything but alone. While I am being paid to doze, hundreds of people mill quietly around me, as if I'm a mossy rock in the river and they are the current. I'm lower than them, in my chair, but they never trip over me. I notice their eyes skim the surface me, not even getting to the black suit I'm wearing, the colour of my eyes. If asked five minutes later about my appearance, they wouldn't be able to vouch for my age or gender. I exist in a category other than that of most material objects. But perhaps that is the point. I sit and, unnoticed, notice things.

I notice that the young man and woman at opposite ends of this room are aware of each other, far more than the paintings they appear to be studying. Look at how she moves, self-consciously arching her back, then rubbing her exposed neck. Yawning artificially. He is carefully *not* looking in her direction when she is most able to observe his indifference. And there they go slipping towards the door. It is a secret dance. Even they don't see how much of a dance it is. I hope they can speak to each other later, perhaps in front of a Degas. Degas can have a catalyst effect. I think it's his use of red. Colours, used correctly, can be social lubricants.

And there's the woman who looks like a lollipop lady. Her face is droopy, soft as if tired from decades of kindness. She'll have a Tupperware container full of shortbread sitting in a pristine cupboard at home. She's frozen in front of the Rembrandt again. Staring. Quite common, people returning to their favourite portraits. Just because someone is dead, doesn't mean you can't have a relationship with them. The rooms with landscapes have fewer lingerers; people flow steadily by meadows and mountains. It's the faces, and especially the *eyes*, they stop for. Lollipop Lady is still staring. I notice the Rembrandt woman's face vaguely echoes her own, and detect a query in the angle of Lollipop's pose. Maybe she is looking for resonance, for answers to her own dilemma. I can understand that. Why shouldn't Lollipop's answer be in the black eyes of this Renaissance woman, painted in a dark and freezing parlour in Holland? Perhaps some eyes can pull our truths out of us in a way nothing else can. Or has Rembrandt wrought some miracle, his model not really powerless and gone. By entering Lollipop's consciousness, she may, in a sense, live on. No one knows these things, do they?

I feel fidgety today. I'm going to re-cross my legs again, and it's only 12.35. There's that man again, grey jumper, heavy-framed glasses, the one pretending to read the plaque below the Renoir. I have a mute rapport with him. He's only here because he perceives it as a wholesome place to spend his lunch hour, when in fact he is so lonely he reeks of it. Loneliness smells like sea water and fermenting grain. Sour and sad, like clothes that have been left on the line in the rain too long and will need to be washed again. This man aches for ordinary human interaction but is too shy to tap into it, so he comes to a place where solitude is the norm. Look at the stiff set of his shoulders, his inability to make eye-contact even with a portrait painted centuries ago, his need to read the words instead. It's obvious he hasn't the first clue how to make small talk. Perhaps he never learned because his wife did all that, and now she is gone. Dead, or away to a more outgoing man, or to that kind of independent eccentric life some middle-aged women aspire to. Ah, there he goes, in his slow-paced walk intended to fool folk into thinking he is like them – here for the art, not the refuge. The irony is that hardly anyone is here for the art.

There are no signs forbidding talk, yet this is mostly a quiet place, a soothing place. Like church, or a library. So I am startled when a woman with an East European accent suddenly barks to an intelligent looking young man: "You have sat on my bag!"

He leaps up from the bench and apologises, though his expression is bewildered as there is no bag on the bench.

"It does not matter you say sorry. You have sat on my bag!" she insists. Her voice is so manly and her face so made up. Maybe she *is* a man. Or this is a virtual reality show and we're being secretly filmed for TV.

"But there is no bag," whispers the man, backing off.

"Ha! You tell me there is no bag, when you have sat right on it!"

I feel sorry for this young man, his gallery calm is shattered, and as he passes by me I try to catch his eye. But he doesn't notice me or my empathy, and it tumbles away, wasted. "Fucking loony Pole," he mumbles.

A mobile phone begins to ring, its ringtone a song: *My Favourite Things*. I feel everyone in the room twitch with irritation and, one second later, they're singing the words in their heads. *Raindrops on roses and whiskers on kittens*. No-one is enjoying the song; it's a cultural reflex. If you were about to be executed, married, or cut the cord of your first-born in some over-heated hospital room, you'd still sing these words if you heard the tune. Sing away in a private room in your head that has a mind of its own. *Brown paper packages tied up with string*. A man, full-lipped and well-fed, finally locates his phone and hisses into it: "I can't talk now. We need to see this man Jacob – he brought in ten kilos."

There is a silence. At least eight people hold their breath and freeze.

"Just stay put. Don't move. Don't answer the door. I'll be fifteen minutes. Ten." This man becomes the only person who notices me this month. He darts me a furtive look that stops my breath. I don't know what frightens me more – my sudden visibility or the ominous one-sided conversation.

Everyone begins to breathe again and move away in an unhurried waltz, as if they're the original atoms that flaked off the skin of the painter. In their imaginations, they're being followed and threatened in dark lanes, or see the kilos of heroin stashed in a derelict warehouse while rats gnaw away at Jacob's corpse. Or they're already editing the story to entertain friends later over dinner and a glass of chardonnay. Two long minutes later – I often study my watch, so I know about time, how it ebbs and flows and sometimes stops altogether – all the tension has evaporated. The room is, for a second, blank.

Then onto this pristine new canvas walks my dream woman. Inches from me! My knees feel an electric jolt where they almost touch her legs. I've seen her before. Oh God, do I look alright? Not overtly bald and fat and middle-aged? Glad I polished my shoes, I sit up straighter and gaze alertly into the middle distance, aiming for a dignified yet reflective pose. I press my lips together and slightly squint my eyes, as if I am finding my own thoughts amusing. This is turning out to be such an important day. Not that any day is insignificant, but this woman – she is making this day … memorable. She was beautiful once, you can tell by her walk, but now I look closer I see her eyes have that glutted look. Almost vacant, spilling over with a surfeit of colours and images, textures, ideas and feelings. Too much oil on canvas. People feed on art, but you can get drunk and insensible, spending too much time here. Why do you think I avert my eyes, even nap? It's not good to look too long, and some people, like this woman, (I imagine her name's Elizabeth. Not Lizzie. Not Beth.) are more susceptible than others. People who are open, for whatever reason, should avoid extended periods in museum rooms.

I know what she'll do now. She will head to the café, this intoxicated Elizabeth, long before she has gone through all the other rooms. They are laid out like a maze and will make her feel dizzy, and soon she'll feel it's not good any more, being here. She'll go to the toilets first, look at her face in the mirror and inwardly wince at the contrast between her inner and outer image. She'll ask herself why she comes here. Why indeed? This woman belongs to a recognisable tribe, and I love each and every one of them. They have woken up late to life and beauty only to be saddened by it. I would easily marry them all, if they'd only look at me.

Maybe the next time she comes into my room, I'll ease off my cloak of invisibility. She'll not be aware I have done this, but will notice me and ask me the time, or the way to the Van Goghs. It will be as if she has broken a spell. I will exist! Her reward will be my generosity and gentleness, and later, after we've imbibed enough wine and walked through enough midnight gardens, she will benefit from my immense well of passion.

"Oh yes!" she'll whisper. I've been watching you for such a long time. Did you never see me? I have been watching and waiting for you!

She will never understand that the opposite has been true. It has been me who has lived in abeyance till her eyes lit on mine. This is a possibility. It is something I imagine, so it can happen. I don't believe in rushing things, but sometimes events rush towards you and I feel capable of rash acts. I do. There are so many yawning voids in the world, for absent mothers, fathers, lovers, friends, cocker spaniels, arm-chairs, cinnamon toast made 'just so' – people are sucked into these voids unaware of anything but the most superficial of explanations. Small children have been sucked into puppy vacuums, giving their puzzled parents a lot of grief; returning soldiers have disappeared into a vortex of widows grieving for other soldiers. I have a romantic love vacuum around my heart, and may pull a woman into my orbit. She will have lived with a love vacuum around her heart too, and probably for a very long time. I believe in the possibility of hearts calling to each other in a language unknown to the brains of men. I believe in the intelligence of hearts.

Ah, there she goes. Today is not the day; Elizabeth will not ask me for the time. I shut that door with a satisfied melancholic sigh and let my eyelids slip down. Tune into the wisps of whispered conversations of strangers, sentences with no beginning or end.

Listen – this is what I hear, in between the silences: "… know what you mean. But avocados? I love them, but they're so risky. How many times have avocados disappointed you? I remember when Tom once …"

"… what she said when I asked her if she had any regrets, listen to this, she just sat there looking awful, and said no … I wish I'd bought that …"

"… and Edie always says that, always! But I will remember to meet that train at …"

"… is he? I still think he should get more money. After all, he was …"
These are the noises people make when they have forgotten that they are mortal. Their chatter channels through empty me, makes a single sound, a soporific rhythm. Like waves. I churn them around, taste them and become – not them, but their stories, which are too close for them to notice properly. After a while, below the voices, I hear a cacophony of heart beats and dreams, of moments and hours, of memories and silence.

You know that place between sleep and wakefulness, where the meanings of words, the shapes of objects and people are blurred and joined. I'm still not moving in my chair. My skin tingles on the edge of unconsciousness and my breathing is slow. In. Out. My watch ticks silently, but my pulse notes the vibrations as if they were tolling bells. I am alive in the world, and will go home with all this inside me. Later tonight, when I hear distant sirens and laughter with equal detachment, this human symphony will linger yet, in the grey air of my corridors. Will sit at my kitchen table while I drink my wine. I will hum with it and not feel lonely.

Gary Allen

Black Dog

I too am the black dog
loping out of the desert rubbish dumps

jerrycan breath, the lolling tongue.

I am the one
who follows you to the city gates

a greedy lover, the whore
always one step and more behind

pads hardened on the sharp stones
you throw at a German nightmare.

From the minarets of this fly city
the imams wail across centuries

to the lost souls bleaching in this fiery land.

The slow arms of the overhead fan
turn above the losing spades.

I am the black dog you left back there
in the bogs and pine forests

in that other place

I came over with you on the troop-ship
sweating in the hammock

heart thumping like the engine pistons.

The marble-eyed beggars see me
the tattooed girls dance before me with tambourines
and you know
without looking over your shoulder

that I am really there.

In the North of the Country

There are no crops
all have been destroyed and trampled
by small feet into the ground.

Darkness falls
the women and girls walk the dusty road
to the compound at Bessbrook.

They talk still with drums,
We are Gods

young men, we wait in the forest
we will teach you how to bite your school friends to death
to make mothers of your sisters.

This woman's ten-year-old son
hacked her lips off with a rusty razor-blade –

when the wind blows
her mouth fills with dust
when she eats, the food falls back out.

My child is a spirit now
among the drumlins and the clever brooks

as clear to me as the yellow whins
or the blackbird's neb.

The Perfect Wife

This woman cut the hair of men
an act of love

like washing dust from feet
or folding away the laundry of the dead.

Each head her palm rests upon is sacrosanct
the ley lines of her own land –

the raised scars of lanced boils
the shell-like womb of fragile bone,

the nail wounds of self-sacrifice
are honed beneath her fingertips.

And here are seas that have died of salt
rivers and valleys of ancient doubt:

now her fingers swell in the scissor eyes
her knuckles deformed by fire and ice.

She throws away the year's ripe grain
and ploughs with a steel comb

while the sermon on the wooden-box radio
commands her to always be busy with wool and flax –

yet she knows better the limits of God's sons,
the silver hair fine as a silken shroud.

Icarus

This child fell from a great height
into a tin bath of boiling sheet-water

the girl's grinning face high above him
hanging from the swaying bed-linen

the branches of the Scotch pines.

Women came screaming through the yards,
the pigeon men looked
from the dowelled windows of their lofts –

faraway kings

as the sun burned down
and the body blistered and peeled.

Let us pretend that we are flying
higher than a girl's shoulders

see how small the earth is
contained like a child's perception

the patchwork yards and fields
the blue hills, the encompassing sky –

and then the fall,
the acceleration into pain
the sea of bandages, the blinding light

the ether voice whispering,
step away from the others
and I will clothe you in new skin.

Oceanography

Sometimes a thought will suggest itself:
it is mid-winter, the island ferry is disabled in the harbour
its rusted chain sagging with bladder wrack
the tailgate clanging with the swell.

These rocks are hard and unforgiving
Dissenters' faith, family laws
promises easily given –

great mountains that once roared
and moved to cool in these waves.

Where does the sea take them?
small boats fragile as match wood
out to Faeroese or Icelandic waters

and brings them back again
down deep channels, secret currents,
spewed up all along this shore

swollen bodies, fish eaten faces,
once they were claimed
by the knitting pattern on their jerseys

up here on Torneady Point
girls would sometimes wait up to a year –

imagine, that cold eye fixed upon this expanse
vast and empty as the thoughts in your mind, my love
those little origami napkins
dropped from the end deck of the outgoing ferry.

My thoughts are clear as January
sharp as the wind that howls
through the caverns of the ruined castle –

henna hair, looped earrings, birth marks,
big as the ocean chart
quiet as a prayer, a morning walk along this pebbled beach.

The Polish Girl

Her arms were like thin sails
bronzed by the burning sun

cotton work-sleeves pinned back
sloe black hair gripped loosely

around us were maps and village lanes
and voices I could not hear

the light false upon the pages
the ink dry upon the table

and people moved about and through us
yet everything and all was contained

(the pebble hard shore, the singing wind
the forest folklore, the wheat fields:

polluted water, closed mines
the empty platform

the husband who put her in hospital
for coming home late, the abandoned child)

within the flickering darkness of her eyes,
and what was lost in translation.

First Confession

Maureen Myant

Sister Mary gies me the willies. She's a right funny face on her. Like a chewed-up caramel, my mammy says. Sometimes it's aw smooth an sleekit, but. Like when she talks tae Father Maloney. Maloney Baloney we calls him. So ah canny believe it when, right in the middle of RE, ah puts my hand up an says, "Please Miss, what about number six."

Ah must be barmy, shoutin out in the middle of a lesson an callin her 'Miss' instead of 'Sister' like she aye tells us. When Mental Mickey done that, he ended up peein hissel she was that mad. Ah look down at my desk. It's clatty. There's some words scratched on the wood an ah try an read them: "SiSTr MaRy eATs BaBys." Ah wonder if she eats aulder weans an all.

"Ah yes, Patricia, the Sixth Commandment. Well, number six is a very important commandment and if you break it, it is a *mortal sin*." Her face is aw red an a wee bit sweaty. "Now as I was saying, number seven is – yes Patricia. What is it now?"

"Please, miss, you didny say what number six is."

"Sister Mary, please and it's 'didn't', not 'didny'." Her voice is aw sharp an nasty like chalk screechin on the blackboard.

Sister Mary screeches back: "Thou shalt not commit adultery. Now we really must press on."

Kathleen O'Donnell's got her haun up as well. "Please Sister, is adultery like being an adult?"

"Er, well yes I suppose so."

"Does that mean all adults are committing a mortal sin?" Kathleen says. She's the class sook an she's nearly greetin, so she is. She's fae a dead holy family by the way. She's got two big brothers that are priests.

Sister Mary smiles at her. She must be feart that Kathleen'll tell on her if she's no nice tae her. "Well no, not exactly," she goes. "Only those who commit adultery are in a state of mortal sin."

"But what is adultery?" ah says.

Sister Mary goes tae the back of the class, her long black habit swishin as she walks. She's dead tall – an as skinny as a skelf. My mammy says it's no wonder she couldny get a man. She's mumblin tae herself. Ah'm no sure but ah think she says, "It's not fair", but she canny have cos she's aye shoutin at Mental Mickey if he says that. He says it a lot, cos she's aye giein him the belt. She stops her mutterin an stands up straight like she keeps tellin us tae do. She's dead crabbit. "Adultery is a *mortal sin* because it is being rude to the Virgin Mary."

Relief. Ah thought it was somethin tae dae wi kissing. But ah hufty know for sure, so up goes my haun again, like it's got a life o its ain.

"Please Miss, by rude do you mean like burping?"

Scary Mary glares at me but ah just keep lookin at her an she gies in. "Well, burping *is* rude of course, but that's not what I meant. It's a special sort of rudeness. It's hard to explain to little boys and girls but if you …" she coughs, "Well, if you let somebody see your underwear for example, it's that sort of rudeness." She sits down, takes out her hanky an wipes her face. "Now we must move on. If anyone else disrupts this lesson, I'll get my belt out."

Ah canny move. Ah done a *mortal sin*. Gerry McDowall seen my vest an what's more he's went an tellt everyone. My soul's in danger. Ah'm no really sure what a soul is but Sister says it's white an it gets black spots on it when you do a sin. Mine's must be manky. At playtime they're all round me, shoutin. Even Kathleen O'Donnell an she's aye nicey-nice tae everyone. She comes up tae me an says, "Oooaaa. You're for it Tricia. Your ma's gonny kill you. Nobody else has went an done a *mortal sin*. Ah'm tellin on you."

Ah'm nearly greetin, so ah'm are, "but ah didny want him tae see my vest. You know that. Ah asked you tae haud up the towel when ah changed. He peeped an you let him."

"Ah did not. Anyway you fancy him. You did so want him to see your vest. Ah'm gonnae tell." She says this all up an down:

Ahm - gonn - ae
te--e--ell

Ah want tae hit her big fat face but ah know ah'll just get intae more trouble. So ah bargain with her instead an by the end of playtime she's got my crisps, a thrupenny bit an a promise of a loan of my brand new shoes an ah've got a promise from her no tae tell. "Cross my heart," she says, "an hope to die." Then the bell goes an Kathleen says: "Ah'd like a Crunchie the morra." Crunchies cost sixpence. Where am ah gonny get that?

Ah've been thinkin hard. If you're truly sorry for your sins then God forgives you, even if it's a mortal sin. But you hufty be truly sorry, Sister says. God sees through any pretence. Ah'm sorry, ah really am but it's mostly cos everyone keeps gettin at me an ah think this maybe isny the same as bein sorry for what ah done. It's like ah'm sorry cos ah got caught. Anyway, ah didny want anyone tae see my vest an Kathleen let the towel slip an what's more she done it on purpose so what ah think is she probably done a mortal sin too cos she helped it happen. Ah tellt her this when ah gave her the Crunchie the day. Her face went aw white, then it went pink an her eyes were aw shiny like she was gonny start greetin. Ah don't think she's gonny ask for any more sweets.

Tomorrow's my first confession an ah've been practisin what ah'm gonny say. Ah'm gonny slip in the adultery at the end after aw the other sins. "Bless me father for ah have sinned. This is my first confession. Ah have been disobedient twenty three times an ah have told fourteen lies an ah stole sixpence from my da an ah done adultery once." Ah shouldny hufty say about the stealin cos that was Kathleen's fault. Ah took the money from my daddy's coat pocket an ah felt dead mean doin it. Worse than ah've ever felt. Ever. Ah hate her, so ah do.

My daddy's takin me tae church so's ah can do my first confession. Ah wanted my mammy tae come as well but she couldny cos she's still making my dress for the morra. She's been making it for weeks but it's no ready yet. My daddy wisny pleased, "An hour or two, that's all it'll take. You should be there, Betty."

We walk down the road thegither. My daddy's no sayin much so ah keep quiet. Just as we're leavin our street we meet Billy from next door.

"Where are the pair of yous goin?" Ah tells him we're away tae church.

"Say a prayer for me," he says an gies me two bob. Ah'm fair chuffed but my daddy disny look pleased. He just says, "No need for that, Billy," an tells me tae give him it back. But Billy willny take it. So my daddy says, "Well, thanks very much," but he still disny sound happy. He's awfy quiet all the way down the road.

The church is full of people but ah only see Father Maloney. He's a very important priest, the high heid yin, my mammy says. He knows lots of things. He can see the Virgin Mary just by closing his eyes an he sees tears runnin down her face because of our terrible sins. Once he came intae our class an tellt us about a man who didny believe that Holy Communion was the body of Christ. So he took the host home an put it on his dressing table. Then he took out a knife an said, "If this is the body of Christ, where is the blood?" He cut it open an *blood came oot!* The man fainted, so he did, an when he woke up he was very sorry an became a very good Catholic. But he made the Virgin Mary cry. Father Maloney seen a great big tear run down her face. He asked us if we could see her an Kathleen said, "Yes Father, ah can see her", aw smarmy like. He gied her a big smile an said, "Ah yes, Kathleen O'Donnell, you are indeed a very good girl. God bless you!" – an he made a sorta wave over her heid with his hauns. For a minute ah thought he was gonny hit her, but he missed. Then he turns round an says, "You others, you need to try harder. Close your eyes and look into your souls and you will see her. Do you see her, boys and girls?" An they aw shouted, "Yes, Father Maloney," but ah seen nothing except they red swirls that you get if you shut your eyes too tight. Ah'm dead feart of him. He's even more scary than Sister Mary. What if ah hufty tell him my sins?

It's dark in the church an there's a funny smell, like perfume but warmer. Ah asks my daddy what it is an he's says it's insects. They burn insects in a dish for Benny Dixon. That doesny sound like a nice thing tae do. There's a man at the door, Mr Murray, an he smiles an winks at me. "Your first confession, eh? Now don't go frightening the priest." There's loadsa grownups standin around an they laugh. "Nae chance," says one of them an ah hide my face in my daddy's coat, wishin they'd gie us peace.

My daddy pushes me through the door, "Let's get it over with, hen." Ah go up the aisle lookin for the smallest queue. That'll be Father Maloney's queue. That's cos he gives out the longest penalties, no, that's no the right word … penances that's it. Really hard prayers like the confetti that nobody knows an if he doesn't ask you tae say that, it'll be three decks of the rosary. Other priests just ask if you're sorry an tell you tae say a Hail Mary or maybe two, if you're really bad. Ah'm lookin an lookin an ah still canny see a small queue. They're aw the same size. Ah close my eyes, "Please God, let me choose the right queue. Let me get Father Craig." Father Craig's funny. He waggles his ears during mass tae make the altar boys laugh. But cos ah've got my eyes shut ah don't see Sister Mary as she comes up behind me. She shoves me intae one of the pews. Ah can feel her finger pokin intae my back, like a pencil. "Move yourself Patricia," she says an ah fall intae the lap of Mental Mickey an he pinches me, right on the soft bit of my arm, but he's no gonny see *me* greetin.

Ah don't like it inside the confession box. There's a horrible smell like the smell off Mental Mickey's clothes: auld food an cigarette smoke an a wee bit of jobby. Ah'm bokin as ah kneel down.

"Are you all right, child?" says a quiet voice. It's too soft tae be Father Maloney an it's no Irish like Father Craig. Ah don't know who it is.

"Take your time," he says.

Ah open my mouth but ah canny remember the words.

"Is there anybody out there?" It's a smiley voice, makes me feel better. "Yes, Father, but please Father. Ah can't remember the words."

"Never mind, use your own. God likes you to use your imagination."

Ah breathe out an the words come in a rush. Ah'm speakin like someone in a film. "Bless me Father for ah have sinned. This is my furst confession. Ah have been disobedient twenny three times an ah have told fourteen lies an ah stole sixpence an ah done adullery once."

"Are you American?"

Ah like my new voice an ah want tae say 'sure' but ah mustn't tell lies in confession. "No Father," ah says. "Ah'm urny."

"Mmm. Tell me about this 'adullery'. What did you do exactly?"

No! He's no supposed tae do this. He should be sayin some Latin words tae cure me of my sins an then ah've tae say a good act of contrition an get my penalty an it'll be over. Nobody tellt me ah might hufty talk about it. *It's no fair.*

"Gerry McDowall saw my vest," ah mutters.

"I see. How did this happen?"

"Please Father, we were in the class an the teacher told us tae change for PE an Kathleen was holding up a towel so's ah could change an she let it fall an Gerry saw an he tellt everyone."

"And who told you it was adultery?"

"Please father, Sca … Sister Mary."

He does a big sigh then, like he's dead tired. Then he says, "No, that's not adultery. It's not a sin of any kind, it's a mistake and Gerry McDowall is a very silly little boy. Now tell me why you stole sixpence."

So ah tells him all about Kathleen an how scared ah'd been that she'd tell my mammy an daddy what ah'd done. He lets me talk an then he says that Kathleen was a naughty girl an ah mustn't steal again. He's so nice ah can feel my soul gettin all shinin bright again. It's great. Ah canny wait for the morra.

My mammy's finished my dress an there's something else – a blue velvet cloak, with a hood. It's lined with a white shiny material that my mammy says is called satin. My dress is lovely – wee puff sleeves an a petticoat that makes the skirt stick out. It's much nicer than Kathleen's.

The only bad thing is that one boy faints. His mammy says it's because of the fastin. Ah'm a wee bit scared that the communion host'll stick tae the roof of my mouth but it doesny. An there's no blood leakin out either.

Ah'm dead happy when ah get home. There's loadsa people in the hoose. Mammy, daddy, nana an granda, aunty Jean an her weans. Loadsy people. Even people from our street who don't go tae our church, like Billy next door. An there's presents. A pair of rosary beads, a missal covered with white glistenin stuff that my mammy says is mother of pearl – an best of all, a bracelet with gold hearts. Ah put it on my wrist an hold it up tae the light. It's all sparkly in the sun, like the wee golden hairs on my arm. "What present do you like best then, Tricia?" says my nana.

"The rosary beads." Then ah remember the nice words that the priest said an ah'm no gonny tell any more lies so ah says, "Well, maybe the bracelet." Nana laughs as if ah've made a really good joke an ah join in.

"Och, it's great tae see you so happy," says my daddy as ah open the rest of the presents. "Ah was that worried about you last week. But you're better now, aren't you?"

Ah feel funny, all grown up, an want tae make everyone laugh. "Do you know something, daddy – Ah Thought Ah Done Adultery."

"Oh aye? Listen everyone. Tricia's got something tae tell us."

Everyone looks at me. "Go on then."

"Well, Sister Mary said adultery was something rude like letting someone see your underwear. Ah thought ah done it, because Gerry McDowall saw my vest. It was an accident," ah says quickly, in case they think ah'm really bad. But they don't. They're aw roarin. Granny Murphy wipes her eyes an says, "Dear God, Betty, I think I've wet myself."

Ah'm laughin as well. Ah love this. It's great makin people laugh. Ah says, "Ah'm glad adultery's no what ah thought it was."

"And what's that, Tricia?" says my daddy.

Ah'm jumpin up an down. Ah shout it out, so they can all hear. "Ah thought it was kissin an stuff like mammy does with Billy next door."

Ah don't know what ah've did wrong, but nobody's laughin now.

Gerry Stewart

Ice Moon

Waking in hushed dawn,
corrie-handed and empty as coracles
we lie on the cluttered shore of our bed.

Storm-tossed angels
cut streams of golden light,
our heat melts the scribbles
of a night pen against window panes.

The midday moon rises
through a periwinkle sky.

Cautious wishes are made
on the slink of a marmalade cat,
to weave our way through all obstacles
entangling our lives.

Winter's crystalline air whispers, shatters.
Christmas trees thrown out on kerbs
collapse like out-of-season umbrellas.

We walk on the uncertainty of ice,
aware of every moment's pressure
splintering below the surface.

Only your arm
locked onto mine,
holds us up.

Retreat

We push through the clearing's lattice of branches.
Fog traces swirling tattoos on our exposed necks,
dewy yellowed grasses catch the light.

At our noisy entrance a magpie breaks
into an occasional song of icy dawn, dried berries.

Leaves glaze the damp ground.
Tumbled beneath our feet, stones lie
sprinkled with lichen like autumnal pottery.

To the wind with our whispers
waves race over the loch's surface.

Even deeper among moss-covered trees,
a hidden white stag watches with molten eyes.

Tourists reaching for the hand of an unfamiliar god,
we make a wish on its presence in our travels.

Tonight I will take you across bare fields
with the moon cutting shadows into geometry.

We will pull our fortunes from the depths
of a midnight well, sweet peat-flavoured water
raised to our lips in baptism.

Melancholy

twists down the back stairs,
silver wings folded over a stooped back.

Rain shines on its brow,
when it nods droplets cut through my tired skin.
It drags itself away,
murmuring like a dove
weighing down a telephone line.

Each night it climbs with worn-out,
scuffed shoes
to the roof of the city.
I hear it trip as it passes my door.

Roosting among pigeons and seagulls,
it howls to the gloom
until stars fall into its lap.
It shuffles them
into the gutters and chimney flues.

From my window, I know it has left us
alone with the vacant moon.
Its pacing becomes my clock,
chiming against my flint-hard hours.

In the morning as it sneaks away
cirrus clouds weep from its eyes,
washing clean the front steps
with its curls of hair.

Some days I invite it for tea
just to take in
its sweet, mumbled sunrise song.

It peers past my chipped cups,
teaspoons weighted
with sugarless dreams,
and politely declines.

Dawn barges in
with no remorse.

Hunter Moon

Old skin of the year cast aside,
a husk blown
over rows of turned earth.

Beneath the moon's deep gold shield
I settle on my haunches,
ground myself,
fertile soil beneath fingernails.

Not to wait.

For you have arrived
like Orion in the arc of sky,
your bow slung, no need of snares.

Lured into the open, scenting,
against my nature
I linger in your spill of light.

You capture me, expose
a darker ghost ready to fall
before your soft advance.

I remind you
when the moon rides high
I will take up my wild pelt
and slip into the night
over frosty hills.

But my tracks fade,
seasons pass
until they no longer have number.

I circle
three times three
before your fire.

Fletcher's Fables
David McVey

Gerda Stone didn't like make-believe.

Stories were just … well, stories. There was no need to wrap messages up in sugar-coated tale-telling. Children should simply be told what they needed to be told.

"Och, what harm can stories do?" said Tam Fletcher, her father. "Sometimes I think ye must have been adopted."

Gerda had been determined to protect her daughter, Jessica, from the web of story and imagination in which her father had swathed her own childhood. Her husband, Simon Stone, had been of the same mind. However, when Simon had abandoned her (running off with a screen-writer), Gerda had to return to full-time work in the bank. Her widowed father, retired and willing, often had to be used for child-minding. Then, one evening, Jessica had said to Gerda, "I love Grandad's stories."

"What stories?" Gerda had snapped.

Miserable Angus

In Scotland, long ago, most places didn't have names. People had to talk about 'the street round the corner', 'that high pointy hill', 'the big town with the clock tower thing' or just 'up there'. Finally, a wise King of Scotland decided enough was enough. Places should have names. People in every village and town and city were told to go out and name things.

In Dollar, people were lucky – their village had a name already, but now they had to think about naming all the hills and burns and glens and farms and streets round about them. A group of prominent villagers divided the area into sections and someone was sent off to each section to name everything in it.

One day these prominent villagers were gathered round the map writing on some of the names that had just been made up.

"All that's left is the area around the castle," said the Provost. "The one at the top of that glen with all the trees. Below the big round hill – and that other big round hill. Is there anyone in the village who hasn't named things, yet?"

Mistress Muckhart, who ran the inn, looked down at her list. "It's just Miserable Angus that's left."

"Good," said the Provost. "That'll see the grumpy old soor-face out of our road for a while."

"That's not fair," said Ben Bowie, the Session Clerk, a godly man. "He's a poor, unhappy soul, Angus."

"It'll do him good," said Mistress Muckhart. "Give him something useful to do for a change."

"That's true," mused Bowie. "It might empower him – improve his self-esteem."

"My, Bowie, they're good," said the Provost. "'Empower'? 'Self-esteem'?

Ye should write these down."

So Angus was sent off to the big castle above the glen to name things. He was a bit bad-tempered about it, but, then, he was a bit bad-tempered about everything. A week later he was called back to see the group.

"Well, Angus," said the Provost, "have ye given names to everything?"

"Aye," growled Angus, "I said I would, didn't I? It was rubbish, though. I didnae enjoy it at all."

"Just tell us the names so that we can write them on the map," said the Provost, keeping his patience.

"Right. The big castle – that's Castle *Gloom*. The hill above it is *Gloom* Hill. The big burn is the Burn of *Care*, in the Glen of *Care*. And the other burn," – there was a hint of triumph now in Angus's scowl – "is the Burn of *Sorrow*. In the Glen of *Sorrow*."

"My, the tourists will come flocking here now," frowned the Provost.

Years later, Clan Campbell moved into Castle Gloom, didn't fancy the dreich name and renamed it Castle Campbell. All the other names are still used and are still on the map, but Dollar folk will tell you: if you want to name things, get someone cheerful to do it for you.

"These stories you tell Jessica ..."

"Aye," Tam Fletcher replied to his daughter. "Which ones?"

"Well, that one about the Dollar people naming things."

"What about it?"

"Well ... she believes it."

"Nothing wrong with that. I believe it too."

"You believe it? But you just made it up!"

"Oh, aye. I made it up. But that doesn't mean it isn't true."

The Voyage of the Vowels

Once, off the coast of Scandinavia, there was an island called Olso. The people who lived on the island were happy and cheerful; they fished and ploughed the earth and ate and drank and worshipped and relaxed like any folk. But one summer, Olov, the island's chief lord, told a gathering of his peers: "I am unsatisfied. Our problem is affecting us badly and cutting us off from the rest of the world."

Olov wanted to be known as a great leader and orator, but he spoke in the language of Olso: if he had used English, his words would have sounded to our ears like, "O om onsotosfod. Or problem os offoctong os bodlo ond cottong os off from tho rost of tho world."

The people of Olso only had one vowel. When foreign ships docked in the island's tiny capital, communication was difficult. Some of the islanders yearned for richer modes of expression. Olov decided to approach the Queen of Olso about the language problem. An audience was granted him, and, after he had bowed to her in the presence chamber, he said, "Your Grace, I propose to equip a vessel and voyage to the far seas in search of vowels to enrich our words, our language and our literature. We are a fine people with a proud history and we deserve to express ourselves in beauty and with variety. I come to ask for Your Grace's approval and support for this venture."

Of course, when Olov said these words in the Olson language, they did not sound quite so impressive. Yet the Queen, in her graciousness, smiled on Olov and his plan. "Make your voyage, Lord Olov," she told him, "and I will gift you a hundred barrels of meal and ten barrels of dried fish to exchange for new vowels. And when you obtain the vowels, be sure to convey the good wishes of the Royal House of Olso."

Olov gave a solemn salute as he acknowledged the Queen's bounty. "No ruler of any land," he said, "would refuse such a generously-given treasure, for all the vowels in the world."

Preparations for the voyage began. Olov drew heavily on his own people for the crew of the galley. They were strong, skilful fishermen who knew the ways of the sea and the handling of the trim little Olso ships. Strong men from the island's interior carried the Queen's gifts and other supplies into the hold. Yet some voices dissented. Many of the women, especially those who were saying farewell to husbands or sons, questioned the wisdom of the voyage.

"It is one thing for our menfolk to risk their lives in search of fish for food, or to defend us in battle," said Holgo, wife of Bodo the Helmsman, "but to voyage into unknown seas simply to gain more and longer words? Pah! Men are such fools!"

"Don't say that, my fine one," said her husband. "I will bring back fine, glittering new sounds for us to speak of our love to each other, and you will have new, richer words to teach our children!"

Holgo just stomped off with their five children.

And there was Kolmon, the finest poet on Olso, a maker of dark, bitter tales of island life. His poems told of the island's harsh life in stark prose that suggested the island's sharp, rocky shores. "Enough of this talk of new vowels!" he would say. "One vowel was enough for my father, and your father, Olov, and yours, Bodo! Why should we be like the nations around us and covet new, fashionable, *chic* sounds? Our language is hard and rocky and sparse, like our island. Yes, we have only one vowel: but it is *our* vowel!"

But the excitement of the voyage had gripped the island, and Kolmon's voice was scarcely heard. On the day of departure, the people of Olso crowded around the tiny harbour in the island's capital. Kolmon remained alone in a little inn outside the town, forming a poem about a man who found and shaped stones, making each one into the same shape.

Olov agreed to return in time to help the older islanders with the harvesting. Then they set sail to the sounds of cheering from the crowd, but by the time the sails were cracking in the offshore breezes and the island was a dark line on the horizon, the sound had died to what sounded like weeping. The sea was calm at that summer time of the year. The ship made good speed, and Olov set course for the south-west where he knew were populous lands, and shipping lanes where they might hope to trade for vowels with other crews.

After two days they spied a modern, steel vessel, low in the water, making slow progress under a cloud of smoke. The ship allowed them to come alongside and Olov asked for a meeting with the captain. He climbed up the rope ladder thrown to him, and was shown onto the bridge. The captain was a stout, mournful man who smoked a foul pipe and seemed to be thinking of other things. Olov, unsure how to begin, said, "You have a fine ship, captain."

There was a flicker of interest from the captain and other officers. "Fine, you say?" said the captain, after interpreting the mono-tonal Olson language, "Fine?" The other officers murmured to each other and one scribbled briefly in a notebook. Suddenly, the captain remembered Olov and asked what he wanted. Olov, conscious of his limited language, explained their mission. "I understand your language," he concluded, "but it is so much richer than ours. Please, we have dried fish and meal to trade. Let us have some of your vowels."

The foreign captain sighed and smiled ruefully. "I wish I could help you. I do. But I am on a voyage on behalf of my people too. We cannot describe or evoke things and we have no literature to speak of. I have been ordered to sail the seas and return with a store of adjectives and adverbs. Our hold," he jerked a thumb towards the huge gulf that lay open for'ard, "awaits our haul."

Olov took his leave of the captain sadly. Soon the steamer without adjectives was a column of smoke on the horizon. "Perhaps Kolmon was right," said Stovod the navigator to Olov. "After all, we can describe the scene we can see in this gathering dusk with the steamship on the horizon, but they, with all their vowels, cannot."

They sailed for many more days and met many more ships, but none had vowels to trade. Some shabbier vessels did express interest in the cargo of meal and fish, and Olov and Stovod were taken into opulent state rooms on board. The purser of the vessel would produce a small treasure chest, unlock a safe on a bulkhead or take them to a strongroom. But once each secure place was open, they did not see the vowels they hoped for. The people seemed to value gold, silver and coins and gemstones more than they valued their words.

Gerda went into the room when the story was finished. "How can you fill a ship's hold with vowels? Or adjectives?" she asked. "They're not real things."

"You enjoyed that story yourself when you were Jessica's age."

"I've grown up," said Gerda, and took Jessica through to the kitchen for tea.

Kirsty's Imagination

"Och, what an imagination you've got, lassie!" said Kirsty's mum.

Kirsty frowned. 'Imagination' was a big word. She tried to picture it in her

Illustration by Shona Dougall

head and saw a kind of large animal, like an elephant, that ate huge meat pies and lived in a giant wooden box.

Her mum meant that Kirsty was able to picture things in her mind. When Kirsty looked at some trees – even the sorry ones at the bottom of her street that were surrounded by dumped rubbish and litter and had spray-paint slogans on their trunks – she saw a magical forest full of strange, glowing beasts, mighty knights on horseback and fairy princesses with special powers. If she saw a river, to her it was a majestic stream on which kings and queens passed by in elegant galleys powered by oarsmen in richly-embroidered uniforms. Kirsty saw colours in words and twisting, coiling shapes in the days of the week and always tried to think up stories about people she met.

"Is that a bad thing?" said Kirsty. "Should I have an i-ma-gi-nay-shun?"

"No, no, ye don't need to worry about it," said her mum. "Imagination is one of the most precious things ye can have. Lots of people lose it as they get older. They should protect it – like a treasure."

Kirsty worried she might lose this precious thing. She had a little wooden box where she kept hair clasps and combs and she took this, emptied it out on her bed, and decided that from now on she would keep her imagination in it.

You can't see or touch or hold your imagination like you can an egg or a stone or a glove. But Kirsty believed she had stored her imagination safely inside. Her treasure was now safe in its own treasure chest. But what if a burglar broke in and stole the box? She'd never get her imagination back then. Now it seemed so important for her to keep it until she grew up. So she decided it was better to do without it for a while to keep it safe until she really needed it.

Early one morning, on her way to school, Kirsty took the box to the trees at the end of the street. She cleared away the grass and plastic bottles and sweet wrappers and dug a hole with a piece of scrap metal that was lying nearby. She buried the treasure box in the hole and hauled an old rusty pram on top of it. Then, leaving her imagination buried behind her, she went to school.

Now for Kirsty a stone became just a stone, a tree just a tree, and when she looked at the world she saw the same sad, shabby place, spoiled by people and their doings, that the rest of us see.

All little girls grow up, and Kirsty did too. She became very clever, able to count and list and organise and put things in their correct place. She took a very responsible job in a big warehouse that sold things made of wood. One day, her manager took her aside and said, "Kirsty, you've done some great work. Everything's now in its place and neat and ordered. The only thing you need is to be more creative. You need to show more imagination."

Kirsty thought deeply: this was the time to get her imagination back. She now lived in the city, and would have to travel back to her home town to dig up the treasure box. After work she took a train back there, left the station, walked up the hill and turned right into her old street. But she stopped halfway down the street, long before she reached the trees – because the trees were no longer there. Instead, there were houses with people sitting in their gardens, washing cars and mowing lawns while their children played. The trees, the rubbish, the litter, her treasure chest, all had gone.

Kirsty travelled back to the city sadly. She had lost her imagination, just as her mother had warned she might.

"I wonder if anyone found it?" said Jessica.

"Found what?" said her Grandad.

"Kirsty's imagination. Maybe one of the builders found the box."

"I hope so. Eh, Gerda?"

Gerda made a face and went into the kitchen. She found a pen and writing pad, and began to write a list of things to buy at Tesco.

"Mind you," said Grandad to Jessica, "it just shows you should keep your imagination handy, nearby, so's you can get a hold of it when you need it."

"Another story, Grandad!"

"Och, lassie, d'ye think I'm made of stories?"

Kenneth Steven

The Slide

We longed for the sharp crinkle of December stars,
that ghostly mist like cobwebs in the grass,
ten degrees below zero.

After the snow came petalling from the skies,
settled into a deep quilt, the frost
diamonded the top, making a thick crust.

On the long descent of the lawn
we made our slide, planed the ground
hour after hour till it smiled with ice.

At night we teetered out with buckets,
rushed the water down the slide's length
in one black stain.

Next day the slide was lethal,
a curling glacier that shot us downhill
in a single hiss.

Even after the thaw greened our world again
the slide remained written in the grass
as long as our stories.

May

We were coming home
on a day that swung between sun and thunder.
Sometimes the road awoke and glistened,
the song of blackbirds in the open windows
like wet splashes, warm and soft.
And as we drove those last hills
something in my mother broke,
opened like a wound.
She stopped the car, her face all glassy,
in the huge banging of the wind.

Against that whole May sky she cried
so small against the hills;
because my father was not there,
because they could not see, together,
the whole year greening into summer –

larches, birches and the lambs with catkin tails.
I sat hunched in the car, hearing the huge waves
that tore from her, for all the years they loved, and wondered –
Do we grow wise in grief,
and where do all its rivers go?

Tobermory

August and the warm rain
rubbed the sky like soft hair.

All around the bay
a ring of smudged blue houses.

Out in the shallows, yachts and masts
breathing up and down and up.

At nightfall you and I circled
the whole horseshoe of the harbour

listening to songs from upper rooms,
Gaelic, and laughter from deep red windows.

The rain, gentle as felt, touched our faces,
webs of rain that came in fingertips

as the dark swelled like a bruise and the bay filled with candles,
and we walked home, talking of nothing and everything

in the soft blue rain
and the rising of the moon.

Columba

It was another day. The bell echoed,
a coracle came with news of Ireland
and a fine cut of meat. The sea
wrapped the island in a mantle of silk.

Everything he did was, as always, a beat slower.
But they saw nothing; the talk was generous,
the laughter easy, as a lark spun songs
somewhere out of sky that still morning.

Yet the horse came. In the middle of it all,
and the faces turned like full moons
as that long head rested on his shoulder
and the nostrils, full of hay, flared.

For the horse, dark in the drumbeat
of his heart, had heard
that edge of death, and wept
softly against the old man's head.

Salt tears like the water that brought him once
out of the heart of Ireland,
would take him now over a last sea,
into the land he had lived.

Suilven

A monster of a mountain;
that great head stretches westwards,
two thousand feet of sleeping,
billowed and battled by cloud.
But for moments when light breaks –
a tipped avalanche of shining –
whelms and burnishes the sides,
turning the scales of this ancient dragon
into finery, into silver treasure.

We were below the head of Suilven
on a day thundered with cloud
above a loch and the blown crests of its waves
when we heard the divers calling and stretching,
aching over wide water. Their voices carried
eerie and long, beautiful, a whole language
borne by the wind of that early August
so we had to stop and listen, our own words
blown away, forgotten.

Who knows how long we stayed, beyond time,
a little of our lives lost and left behind, still listening.

The Music

He got his tunes that way;
he heard them,
as though they were edges of wind,
as if he saw the notes
in the loud rattle of the storm,
in the darkness, coming out of nothing.
He listened for them, as though they were bees

in ones and twos to begin with,
then a swarm, a black net, a mist.
He had to catch them in the bow of his fiddle,
he had to find them before them passed,
were gone and lost forever.

Where had they come from, those notes?
It was as though they had been sent to find him
through the rampaging of Atlantic gales,
or else had blown off course
like a ship's cargo, like a pirate treasure hold,
had spilled onto St Kilda, into his hands,
into the fiddle,
till it was filled brimful.

He wrote none of them down.
He caught them when they came;
he caught them in the net of his listening,
recognised and remembered them,
stored them in his head as the others
stored fish and birds for winter.
They lay in the dark of his head
like gold in the depths of a cave.
They died with him too
the day his eyes glazed and their light
failed and faded for ever. The tunes were blown out
and back into the wind.

The Poet

Remembering George Campbell Hay

He heard it at low tide from the fishermen,
in the frail morning light before school
as he stood at the top of the beach, all sore with cold,
and a heron beat across the bay in slow rags.

They threw it to each other, whole ropes of Gaelic,
bright, fine lengths of it with such strange knots.
He crouched, knees up, in the lee of the wind
and caught the strands, fiercely, held onto them.

He kept those few fine threads of language,
the bits blown in from the boats,
and built from them a building –
a place to give birth to words.

The Drowning

Saint James Harris Wood

Perhaps I am put in charge of the three-year-olds because it is believed that we are all equally unbalanced. Separately, Lowell and Little Larry are untamed but manageable. Together, never still or short of bad ideas, they easily wear down the average adult. The boys run maniacally everywhere, frequently throw their clothes and shoes out bus windows, are well known patrons of the Emergency Room, had only recently learned to talk and were still liable to communicate by grunting, miming agony, barking, or any of a dozen non-verbal modes. As Lowell's dad and Little Larry's uncle, I'm the only one in our extended family with patience for their shenanigans. Acting out, yelling and crying mean nothing. The rule of thumb declares that if no one is bleeding, then everything is OK. One school of thought thinks badly of my parenting skills, and the most asked question from that quarter is: 'Can you control those kids?'

No. We go on expeditions all over San Diego to avoid condemnation. My chronic unemployment is also a factor as I want minimal contact with relatives and well-meaning busy bodies who have a vested interest in harassing me. The boys and I roam the city on long bus rides to movies, record stores downtown to study the downtrodden, or wherever the moment's notion dictates.

Last week we ended up on the half-mile pier off Ocean Beach. The pier looks to be at least fifty years old and is favored by fishermen, couples and lollygaggers. It's a rickety affair shaped like a giant T, wide as a normal suburban street, with three-foot high splintery wooden guard-rails.

We arrived near dusk at the end of an exhausting, overcast day that hadn't worn the boys down in the slightest. As was their custom, they took off and had been to the end of the pier and back before I'd walked a third of the way. Both have reputations as nationally-ranked runners. Not for speed so much, though they are quick, but for endurance and the number of escapes. Their school pictures are posted at the local mega-mall in the security offices where numerous episodes are documented. At one point the boys' mothers, Diane and Carol, gave me actual leashes. Like a fraud, I strolled through the mall while Larry hung his head, moaning as if recently tortured, and Lowell yipped and snarled, straining at his leash, acting the fool. Yet the very minute when I released them out of compassion (while admonishing in the most threatening manner, 'Stay!?'), they single-mindedly trotted off exactly like the Australian aborigines who jog across the continent with little provocation.

Luckily, the boys are conditioned to a small degree and usually head straight for Toys R Us or the bookstore. Unluckily, these establishments are at opposite ends of the mall and it can take 15 to 20 anxious minutes to track the wayward youth. Also problematic is the endless diversity of mall distractions available to sidetrack quick-to-wonder three-year-olds.

Once, when they escaped because I blinked, I spent a worried hour's search before going, reluctant and shamefaced, to security, who had only contempt for anyone outwitted by children. The boys were in custody, eating ice cream, after having been captured in front of Nordstrom's taunting actresses whose craft led them to work as living mannequins. "Are you dead, lady? Are you dead?" the boys asked repeatedly in classic toddler fashion until the manager of the store called for backup.

So, seeing Lowell and Larry trotting off in the distance, down the pier, wasn't alarming. I did pick up my pace, more than I liked, trying to keep up. The day grew late and other than ourselves I saw only an old grizzled fisherman casting off the end of the pier, and a young couple walking arm in arm back towards shore.

Waves were high, salt water sprayed the nippy air. The boys again made the end of the pier and were nearly back to me. They stopped, and both tentatively put a foot on the lower slat of the railing, pretending to climb, testing, knowing I'd yell, "Get the hell off there!"

They ran circles around me laughing and piping, "Hell, hell, hell!" assimilating the word into their vocabularies – and then took off, running.

"Don't curse! Stay off the rails!" I shouted, unheard, into the wind. Finally at the end myself, I peered at the ocean. Large waves, turbulent and dirty, marched to the beach. The sky acted as if it wanted to rain and the sun touched the horizon. I studied the agitated scene for thirty seconds, one minute tops. Turning around, only the old fisherman was in sight. A quick jolt of alarm took away my breath.

"Lowell! Larry!" I yelled, in a strangled, mean, dad voice. Looking down the length of pier towards shore I couldn't see anybody. The boys were fast, but in no way could they have made the shore.

Now frightened, I ran from one end of the cross bar part of the pier to the other, mindlessly studying emptiness. There was no place to hide and the boys were nowhere in sight. Moaning deep in my chest, I hurried over to the old fisherman, still casting his line.

"Did you see two little kids? "I'm sorry to bother you, but I lost a couple of kids."

"Ye'r the one lost."

The old man had hunted fish for so long that he'd turned barbaric. Ignoring him, I leaned over the rail and studied the dark waves. Mounting terror, many times that of any I'd felt at the mall, clawed at my heart.

Turning in a quick circle, frantically looking in all directions, it dawned on me that there was nowhere but in the water to look. On the verge of crying and unable to draw a good breath, I desperately latched onto the idea that the boys might of somehow crawled down below the boardwalk. Lunging under the bottom slat of the guard-rail, I bumped my head and skinned a cheek, then leaned precariously out over the water in order to look beneath the pier.

The fisherman growled in disgust, "Ya idiot! Ye'r gonna fall in. Ye'r scarin the fish."

"My kids are gone! Do you understand!?"

"Ye'r overreactin."

"Bastard!" I whispered explosively under my breath, then leaned even further, studying the underpinnings of what I now recognised as a death trap. The pier's infrastructure held no sane pattern. Dark and filthy, covered with the dead bodies of sea creatures misfortunate enough to be caught in the evening's rough sea, it smelled of death and rotting seaweed. Some of the pillars were obviously rotten and broken and had no business being there. Waves smashed against the apparatus, clearly trying to destroy the pier.

There were no children.

"Larry!! Lowell!!!" I screamed, frightening a cancerous albatross that must have been an imbecile to live under the godforsaken pier. The daft creature, darkly covered with dirt and oil, on second inspection resembled a large disoriented bat. Regardless, it flew at my head, croaking piteously, its vile wing brushing my face, nearly caused me to plunge into the sea and die like everything else. Catching my balance and pulling up quickly, I smashed my back into the guard-rail and almost fell in again. The old man grabbed my foot, cursed me and unceremoniously yanked my body back onto the boardwalk like a fish.

Scrambling to my feet, I bayed at the sea, "Lowell!! Larry!! Lowell!! Larry!!"

"This is hard to believe," the old fisherman said.

Completely unhinged, staring at the ocean, now darker than ever as the sun had nearly set, the unthinkable gnawed on me. Lowell and Larry were gone, no bodies left to prove they'd ever lived. Muttering threats and prayers to God, my heart radiated pain. In anguish, I shouted their names over and over.

"Ye'r too excitable. Ye'r scarin the fish."

"The fish are dead, you old fool!" I had no more civility for this savage.

I wanted to strike him but turned away to look madly, in all directions. Spinning helplessly in a circle, nearly witless, losing the will to breathe, a great pressure built on my chest and stomach. Extreme anxiety emerged as a deadly lethargy, my mind and body shutting down in order to flee the circumstances of my irresponsibility. I caught sight of a shape rising with the tide, but it was only a batch of seaweed headed shoreward. The idea planted, of the boys' bodies floating lifelessly, made me choke.

I could not breathe. I love these kids more than myself. Lowell is my first born, and there has never been a better son in the history of such things. Little Larry is smart, funny, and the son of my brother, Big Larry, who lets us stay at his house. If they are dead, I am dead, figuratively and literally when their mothers find out. The very thought of facing their mothers was enough to push me into the sea, even if I had a fabulous life, which I don't. I'm regarded as a slacker by relatives throughout the country. When it circulates that I'd presided over the drownings, every dire expectation and rude comment will be fulfilled. I could never face anyone again. Better to leap in the sea, make a futile rescue attempt, and die smashed against the evil pier.

Hands on rail, I climbed and cried one last time, "Lowell!! Larry!!"

While staggering up and down the pier, a small trash barrel attached to the railing escaped my notice. A chortling sound came from someone hidden between the barrel and the cruel fisherman. I recognised the authors of that chortle. My last agonised cry must have tickled their funnybones. Exposed, the boys jumped out, joyfully dancing, filled with glee at having hidden so successfully, and tricked me so completely.

Paralysed with astonishment and exhaustion, unable to move or close my mouth, I stared. Lowell, hands clasped over head, hopped merrily from foot to foot in an Irish jig of sorts, while Little Larry hooted and did a mambo. It wasn't happiness at being alive – they'd never heard of death. It was simply sheer joyous exuberance born of absurdity.

Grabbing each other's hands, they continued to dance, did some hip hop, square danced, then finally fell to the ground laughing helplessly.

"Why didn't you …?" I asked the fisherman as I climbed down from the rail.

"I wouldn't get involved with those kids – or tell 'em anything."

"Yeah," I said. "Yeah."

The Window

She left me in the middle of the night
Literally it was about a quarter to three
Woke me up when I heard the door slam
Note on the pillow she didn't give a good god-damn
Didn't take anything except the cat

Apparently a boyfriend in Quentin had been set free
My legs buckled as I ran down the stairs
Heard a car cough but no one was there
Heard a siren about fifty miles away
Three a m hoped the cops were chasin' them
I tear her room up find porn and cocaine
Broke the TV she held in such disdain

I stare out the window for hours on end waitin'
To see Jocelyn
She told me about a million times or more
Literally it was all she could see

The injections … that wasn't good
Now she's gone off to Hollywood
Found her poetry and biography on Rimbaud
Efficiently left me in the lurch

My anger like prayers in a church
The stoned glass through which I stare
Shows nothing   everywhere
Empty cars from midnight to noon
Leaving me completely undone
I stare out the window for hours on end

Stands to Reason

Every jack one of us
stands on the Earth which is whirling
at a thousand miles an hour,
constantly.

At the same time the earth
is whirling, it describes an orbit
around the sun at seven thousand
miles per hour.
Simultaneously, the solar system
is spinning in yet another direction
at a rate that Einstein himself
questioned.

While this perilous set of facts occurs,
the galaxy where our solar system resides,
is itself known to cartwheel wildly.
Again, this galaxy is only a small part
of a universe untold millions of light years
across, also moving towards God knows where.
Imaginably, there is probably yet another
even bigger something, that is vibrating,
staggering, oscillating, bounding, confusing –
even further.

How can anyone be expected to keep
their breath or stay on their feet
while being hurled in all directions;
I ask you.

Benjamin Morris

A Trick of the Light

You could have been Sam Spade
but for a trick of the light –
standing there at the mirror, modelling
my fedora, all you would've needed

is a trench and a shadow
to blend into. As it is this room
is too well-lit, this bottle of gin
on my desk far too full

for us to be Bogart and Bacall,
you at the Victrola and me lighting
a Lucky, each of us primping our
banter before we take a drive

down the boulevard of this night.
Look – there, down an alley, a scrap
of paper is fluttering on which
is scrawled a clue to your heart,

a map through these darkened streets
through which I find myself
wandering without a destination,
hoping for a taxi to be sent

to take me where I know I can
find you – standing there at the piano,
singing *And Her Tears Flowed Like Wine*,
eyes alighting past me to the door.

Chiaroscuro

(after a line by Norman MacCaig)

From here the cloud over the reactor
seems set like a jewel in the sky,

and in the seat across from me
the girl with the oyster mouth shuffles

in her sleep. Past her, out the window
I see the shadow of a road within the fields,

slipping over the far ridge the way your voice
at times slips into my drowsy mind.

Were we to dig, what would we find there –
what buried gods, what ochre beads or

slim pendants long rusted away? By the hedge
a few pigs sit sweet-talking the soil;

a cow chews on nothing, then swallows.
With luck the sun will set tonight,

with luck this landscape too will melt
like a mind before dreaming: to feel again

soldiers marching, the night become
a sharp-eyed bird alighting on its nest.

At the Bacon Retrospective

I can almost see what he was looking for,
now that I'm surrounded on all sides
by the inconsolable bulk of them –
panel after panel of lovingly smeared faces,

paintings we had to learn how to call
portraits. Yes, I can see it, the almost
unimaginable simplicity: his dreams,
he was painting them as they came to him

in his dreams, their noses and mouths
swept away into deep emerald and obsidian,
their eyes a russet smear from the mind's
indelicate brush – Am I to tell you, then,

of the dream that I had last night, in which
you came back to me, as you so seldom do now,
am I to tell you some day that when you
finally did return, in a shapeless place

outside the provenance of time, that I was
cruel to you, that I was callous, and hurtful,
and for no other reason than that I thought
it might make you stay, and lash back,

so that I could look at you, and
remember you, so that when I woke,
sharing my bed with shadows, your face
would be whole again, smeared only by weeping?

The Sunset Hunters, Oia

Sun. And sky. And in the sky white clouds.

— Czeslaw Milosz

After it's over they shuffle eastward
down the slim streets as though
the funeral were waiting for them
at the other end. Their chattering cameras
hushed by darkness; their glad claps
when it died, fallen softly into the wind.
So strange to think that they've come
from so far away to watch what happens,
in truth, every day: a pool ball
slipping into its pocket. Are they here
for something else, then – an omen,
a sign in the hollows behind Naxos?
Maria tells me that the sun
never quite hits the sea when it sinks,
that it always founders on its trip home,
there, right there, over that far island
which is slowly beginning to gleam –
as if there were nothing hidden behind it,
no dimly hinted truth that no one
was trying to reach or realise.

Postcoital

Outside, black taxis slick the unlit streets
while we share the last – the lucky – cigarette.
My mind, exhausted from the thankless feat
of satisfying you, cannot forget
the things you said and will not say again.
Cosí è la vita, I used to think
was the Italian *c'est la vie.* But then,
as in so many times, I only drank
the wine I'd set out for myself the thought
before. – Like now, perhaps, imagining
the ways that *is* can fasten on an *ought.*
Ah, ethics, where we learned that everything
was argument, and open to debate,
that the world so rarely waits for those who wait.

A Vocabulary Exercise
Svetlana Lavochkina

"Shall I wear make-up?"

Manya is in front of the corridor mirror to study her face in the bisque lamplight, sallow cheeks and puffy eyes. Manya has been dragging through the chores of the day numbed, in her usual low-battery manner. She has managed to do the absolute minimum, a hair's breadth away from shame. She is accustomed to the incessant drizzle of small embarrassments. Buried in the mud of routine, a soiled jewel, Manya is born to be a ballroom queen, so she firmly believes, and will in due time be washed and polished. Shimmer cubes and crystal balms peek up at her from the dressing table in their colourful yearning. "No. Not tonight."

She whisks the artificial helpers resolutely away. Today, she needs ethereal make-up, not a tangible puff-powder. She looks at the rickety face in the mirror and then beyond it. She finds the dimension where Manya is not a sad clown but a beauty, her lips and cheeks turn rosy, her sharp features soften, and warm amber fills the empty honeycomb cells of her eyes. "Am I pretty now?"

She knows she is. Lit, made over, a hostess-to-be at a secret feast in odd premises. She skulks into the dusk of the bedroom and opens the squeaking wardrobe. Lithe fingers know their tactile way through ferns of fleece and vines of silk. Here it is, a little leaf hidden among piled up clothes, plucked out of the thicket, carried to light, and put to her heart.

"We are going to meet someone," she says to the leaf and hides it in her jeans pocket. Manya is ready to leave, one shoulder perhaps unintentionally bare. She slips into the kitchen to snatch two lumps of dark cayenne pepper chocolate that sends her heartbeat astray. This is a chocolate she doesn't bite and chew but sucks at like a lollipop for fear of pleasure overdosage, or a burn. She slides herself vaguely into the living-room: "Ich komme um Mitternacht zurück." – *I'll be back at midnight*. The opaque figure in front of the TV-set doesn't reply.

She is off, three flights of wooden stairs squeaking more than she would like. It is 9.45. It's snowing outside. Manya accelerates. She feels like an aeroplane on a wet tarmac runway, the plane about to take off. She throws back her head. The windows of the houses on both sides of the street blur into long parallel arrows, multiply, showing the way to her heaven. She is faster than the trams, faster than the buses, and presently flying, higher and higher. Manya's three-dimensional world rests on a German x, a Russian y and an English z.

Her native tongue, her spine, the marrow of her bones is Russian. She treads on the German ground and has been in unreciprocated love with English since she was seven. She tries to breathe with it, but this air is as thin as you'd find high up on a mountain. The words tease, bully and won't obey her and this is why poor Manya is always on the verge of fainting, or bursting into tears. However, she still hasn't given up. She thinks of the loud names of men of letters and whispers a secret prayer she has been reiterating since childhood, "Masters, big and small, dead and alive, admit me to your celestial quarters, I'll polish the parquet floor in your parlours. Don't call me a poet, a poetastrix will suffice, and I will be honoured and humble."

The address she reaches on her winged foot at 10 sharp is an earthly affiliate of the heavenly headquarters Manya yearns to belong to. On a moon-lacquered tablet of a small paved square the little Manya is served a snow-glazed lemon cake of a house. Panting, she shakes off the stray snowflakes from her flaxen frizz and cools her burning face with frozen fingers. She pauses for a second with pounding heart and then touches the Latin name on the plate of names. The bass buzz unlocks the heavy stained glass door and Manya opens it with her shoulder. She doesn't want to switch on the light and gropes her way up the steep staircase, a flour bug enjoying every bit of sweet darkness.

The apartment is agape, the hallway dimly lit. No mirror to check if the imagined make-up is still there. Nobody receives her. She stumbles over an anthill of books, shoes, coats, socks, wires and ancient telephones and alarm-clocks. Seven minutes past ten.

There is a sound of flushing and a door swings open revealing the owner in a veil of toilet air conditioner. "One squatted under a pine-tree," flashes in Manya's head blasphemously, but in fact she is in awe. She only dares to raise her eyes gradually. First they rest on the shabby slippers, then on robust legs shorter than hers, dark green T-shirt, larynx, goatee, moustache, tangled longish hair the colour of the chocolate she's lollipopped, narrow face with plump cheeks and round prune eyes, malicious lips. A male squirrel.

"Hello, Mania," he says. "How are you?"

Manya doesn't correct him. She knows he will never remember how to pronounce her name correctly, and frankly, the name he called her describes her even better.

"Hi, Andrew, I'm fine," an elementary textbook greeting read without enthusiasm. Andrew is Manya's teacher in an advanced conversational weekend course, a genuine American from New England with a Bachelor's degree in English Literature and undoubtedly one of *the* men, big or small. He is witty, and charming, but offhand and a scatterbrain, with an attention span of five minutes. Andrew is a fatal attraction to Manya as well as to many other female students of the evening course. He is her cayenne pepper, her fire, her pure oxygen for thickening the mountain air. Manya has been allowed to visit him in his domain for the first time.

"Go to the kitchen and sit down if you can find a place. I have to make a phone call," Andrew says. "Don't remove my books from the chairs! I'm working," he shouts from the other room.

Manya tries her best not to destroy the spell of random patterns that the books and notebooks surrounding yesterday's unwashed plates, half-empty bowls and saucepans, milk and juice cartons make on the kitchen table, chairs and floor. There is a tiny edge for her to sit on and wait. Wait to unwrap the tribute, the white uncombed mixed-blood lamb she brought her magus, who isn't in the least hurry to attend to his bare-shouldered guest. She sees that the tea is ready, warmed on a table stove, but dares not pour herself a glass.

"You love couscous, Anna, don't you," his nutmeg voice reeks from the other room.

Manya sits still, imbibes the surroundings, as much as she can, omnivorously. The wall clock in the kitchen shows half past ten. Let him 'couscous' Anna all he likes. Manya is here! Every second in the palace is precious. She breathes her oxygen. Her feast continues. In ten minutes Andrew returns, his face a faun mask, and pours Manya some tea with not even a tiny biscuit.

"Shall I help you to clean up? It's such a mess here," she says.

"I love this mess. You don't have to."

The conversation is awkward, the words jumble up and stick in Manya's throat. The elegant questions she prepared at home are forgotten, and some answers to his anticipated queries come out in a hiccup. She realises that she has not the slightest desire to talk about herself or to get to know him better, the more so since Andrew seems unable to concentrate on her petty life. Serve her right. The enamelled cup of his image, too, should stay unperturbed by reality. He puts his foot in a worn-out slipper on the crossbar of her chair. Well, Cinderella's ball is at the point where the prince is to invite her for a dance, or she will invite him if he won't.

"I have something with me. Please don't laugh. I've written a poem."

"I don't know Russian."

"Well, it is … in English. I had something I wanted to express. If you could look at it and tell me what you think of it."

"OK, if it isn't too long."

"Not at all, only fourteen lines, like Shakespeare's sonnets."

"Like Shakespeare's sonnets. Lovely." The voice is impermeably polite, but she senses an undertow of annoyance.

"I'll leave you for a moment, while you read it." Manya, half-mad with anxiety, wades her way to the bathroom, where she finally finds the mirror, but her eyes just can't fix on the reflection. The end rhymes of the poem throb in her head, nearly bursting it.

"… at your feet is black … my love complete … and never back … the sweetest tunes … who knows … your eyes like prunes … she bows …"

The poem rotates its third turn in her blood circulation. Manya stumbles back to the kitchen. Andrew smiles at her in a way she can't interpret. His smiles bear different degrees of malice. She whispers, "So?"

Andrew stands up, cups her nape gently. "You've chosen me for your Dark Gentleman?"

"M-m-maybe."

"What else do you have in your little head?" Manya is stony silent.

"I know what. A lovely mouth. Have you ever played a musical instrument?"

"A flute, at school long ago."

"That comes in handy. Your poem should be accompanied by some music." Dead and alive, they see her! *They* are letting her in! He liked it! The flute is unsheathed, and there is silent music, a faun non-verbal tenor solo, at half past eleven pm, in the kitchen among millions of mute words. Manya is rewarded for her labours and, humbly kneeling, is blessed to be served the cream liquor directly out of the horn of plenty the merciful Masters passes her as a gift directly from the Celestial vaults. She ascends, Andrew descends each to their respective chairs, breathless, now peers.

"Wow, that was wonderful. Where did you learn that?"

Manya is blissfully and reverently silent. She thinks his eyes sink into hers. Prunes in honey fondue.

"Listen, Mania. We could meet from time to time. You're fun. How about next week?"

"And … you did like the poem, Andrew?"

"Oh that. I do appreciate what you have done. A good vocabulary learning exercise. Wait! You have given me an idea. In our next class I'll ask the students to write poems for homework, and use as many new words from that text about pollution as they can. Then you can write another poem with these words. This will improve your English."

The heavenly liquor sticks in Manya's throat and her rosy cheeks turn crimson. "It's nice I gave you an idea," she mutters.

"I tried to write poems in English too. And where I am now? Teaching Present Simple to pleasant insipid Germans. Now will you excuse me, I have to go to bed. I must get up early tomorrow." He yawns broadly.

"Can I stay here, in the kitchen, a while? I still have tea in my cup."

"Sure, but then I won't see you off, too sleepy."

"Oh, you don't have to see me off."

"Then – click the door behind you and komme gut nach Hause. See you around."

He is off, to the bed Manya will never see. She has ten minutes before midnight to burn and extinguish her disgrace. This must be done in solitude, with fireworks in the empty ballroom. She turns off the light and puts a flame to a long candle which is among kitchen utensils. She can't find a candlestick, so drops some wax on the table and fixes the candle in the sticky puddle.

Manya lets the little creased leaf, a larva never to turn into a butterfly, catch fire, and casts it into the sink. She bursts into tears, oblivious of the spiritual make-up she no longer needs, to the books she shouldn't move. She goes to the bathroom and sobs, washes her face, snivels, and washes her face again. "You don't think I'm fit to polish your floors," she hiccups. "Not even scrub your toilets." When the fit subsides, she calls for a taxi. Exit, to the flourish of loud snoring. The ride home in a yellow Mercedes seems much slower than was her flight to the Celestial Quarters.

It's midnight now. The home staircase squeaks unbearably. The figure still in front of the TV doesn't move to meet her. Manya slips into the kitchen to take two lumps of milk chocolate that will now send her, sallow-cheeked and puffy-eyed, to sleep. She will then wake up to her next low-battery day. A bad dancer, as her mother said, will stumble over his own scrotum.

It is five minutes past twelve. The candle in Andrew's kitchen shares its fiery generosity with the multitudes of quick and dead words, Merriam Webster's Dictionary infected first, the words all come alive, scarlet and hissing before cremation.

Tamara Fulcher

San Francisco Tragedy

for the Harris-Greely children

I imagine you told them where you were headed,
and that their legs were picnic keen,
because to them a pier looked like fun on stilts
and not a bridge to nowhere.

Something was calling you
and you called it Voices.
I wonder, but I think God does not need to shout
His summons,
and that the beckon of the waves is not
quite so specific.
But then, you have surely heard a lot
that I have not.

You might have bought them candy.
Time and the autopsy will tell,
if their fat and tiny stomachs are not already emptied
by fish,
the awful downward rock of water.

I can get over what you did – just –
but not that you undressed them.
That you stood them like a row of sorry
and picked their clothes off them,
their solid, unshaded yellows and greens
and ironic blues
until they were stripped, shoulder to heel.

Was it then you told them
you loved them?

(At three and six a boy can speak,
not at one, however;
I guess he looked at you
or the sky.)

I would ask, what did you think afterwards?
Did you look down to check their black float
and think of logs,
observe their hurried sinking,
their final fleeing from your side?

I wonder whether it was as easy as sometimes I imagine,
whether you felt saved.

Creation, after all, is the aching trial with blood,
it takes days;

its opposite is quick:
a decision,
then the push, then the flood.

A Primitive Truth

In actual fact she wasn't gagged.

Lucas had this thing, not to be
bitten but to have the girl pull back her lips to show
her teeth, for him to examine, and if
their white was white enough he would let her
slide it down his skin,
his notion being that she maintain constant contact
whatever snag, whatever trip her mouth might meet.

Matthias helped by holding her head.
He had all her hair, spilling through his fingers;
it made Marcus laugh and say, "You look like you're
grooming a bitch," but Matthias was thinking of his breathing,
the weight of a skull with brain and eyes, which hill and
how well her white was riding.

I called myself Jonas. She said, "Like the whale?"
and I said, "Mammalian, yes. But no. *Jonas.*" Lucas,
though, it was who hugged her, told her what to do and when
she might begin to think of stopping;

Marcus, inevitably, who said he'd heard that noise before,
he thought, in a zoo. "The sound of a startled baboon,"
he concluded, and moved himself, to get a better purchase
on her end.

Love, Being Underemployed (I)

every two or three years
you and I have one long
and significant conversation

and it is like standing for a long
and significant time
in bright sunshine

energising

and I do not think
nor have to
for I know I have you

(see you in 2009)

Love, Being Underemployed (II)

if you were
something
I had worked on for a long
and lonely time

and I were an alchemist

that is how much I want
to put you
between my teeth

Love, Being Underemployed (III)

There are a number of things you have
and need to do
in order to get the best (me)
for you
out of this life (yours and ours).

One, is stop reading Charles Bukowski;
two, is start stalking me, because
I would respond to an obsession; and
three, is book three tickets to Sydney,
Australia.

I have an uncle there, and I would
play with you under a blanket
all the way on the plane.

Why Angus Calder Matters

Thinking about this issue, I couldn't let it appear without tackling the conundrum of Angus. He was a force for good in so many fields, a positive influence on so many, both professionally and personally. Yet there was a downside about which, as I contemplated the world without him over the months and years after his death, I realised that this downside was probably essential as a devilish corrective, keeping him sane and energised in an insane kind of way; it revealed the depths of his humanity, it was the birthing place of his poetry and much else. But I realised too that it might cloud his achievement in the eyes of posterity – hence the present tense – "matters". He did matter; he made a huge difference to Scotland, the UK, and the world at large. He fought literally to the death for all the right things. All here look at both sides of the coin, each contributor with his or her own special involvement with this very special man, for whom we have considerable cause to recognise and thank. (*the Ed*).

Woodland Burial: Angus Calder 1942-2008

Today your face was everywhere: –
in the tilt of a daughter's jaw,
the flop of a son's hair.

I think you were standing a little way behind
watching, as young men shouldered your white box
shoulder-high through the light-green summer trees.

You entered the healing earth to a choral sigh
sent on your way with a woodwind song and a poem.
Only the dram was missing and that came later.

It was a perfect day for cricket.
No Greek wailing. No Celtic keening.
Nobody tore their breasts, their arms, their clothes
None of your former loves clawed rival faces.

A speckled thrush adjusted his civic waistcoat
Cleared his throat and welcomed you to his home.
You lie near a row of Polish generals
And a gravestone inscribed MacDonald,
The Lewis equivalent of Smith

We should warn them, you'll test their mettle,
Already I hear the clack of curling stones
The rustle of manuscripts in the thin air.

Sheena Blackhall

Outside of the Tower

Gowan Calder

When I graduated from drama college in 1990 and returned to Scotland, my father was very much at the centre of my re-introduction to Scottish cultural society. (Not so much a 'coming out' as a sneaking back in Stage Left, hoping nobody had noticed that I'd traitorously chosen to study down south). At that time my father was on the board of both the Royal Lyceum and 7:84, and frequently got invited to various theatre first nights. We often went together – amongst the pros were the free tickets, amongst the cons was the fact that we sometimes saw an awfy lot of shite. But I rarely turned down an opportunity to accompany him, because the pleasure of the evening was often not the play itself but the time spent in the bar afterwards. Yes, of course drink was taken, but the real enjoyment was in the talking. Sad to say, I rarely had any other opportunity to analyse the medium I loved with any real intellectual vigour. These conversations felt subversive, dangerous even, because as my father mournfully pointed out, I had returned to a country where 'intellectualism' was treated in certain quarters with suspicion at best and, at worst, contempt.

We also went to the movies together – a much safer option as there was no risk of being caught looking less-than-convinced by the evening's entertainment by its proud progenitors. We decided, months after its release, finally to 'brave' *Braveheart* together. We sat huddled, watching the smallest screen at the Dominion along with the three other people in Scotland too ashamed to admit they had been avoiding this latest addition to our cultural canon. Dad wrote about this outing later in his collection of essays, *Scotlands of the Mind* (Luath Press 2002). "Scots are cheery. Scots make jokes. Kilted Scots are sexy but Scottish toffs betray prole Scots" was his pithy summary of the three hours of blue-faced, Mock-Jockery we had witnessed. He also quotes one of the better lines uttered by Robert the Bruce in the film: "From top to bottom this country has no sense of itself".

Dad belonged to the Scotland famed for its great thinkers, its scientists, its philosophers and poets – not to a Scotland happy to be perceived as a nation of brightly be-kilted and cheerful *losers*. His greatest desire in life was to help this nation love itself. His greatest fear was that he would appear elitist simply because he was both very well-educated and, quite frankly, extremely clever – one of those 'toffs', sneering at the proles. The irony being, unless there was a pub called The Ivory Tower that I don't know about, I never saw him in one.

I won't lie, over the years my father's propensity to drown his fears with a dram or ten, was the cause of more than one awkward moment. On one occasion he appeared at a rehearsed reading I was performing in and promptly fell asleep in the front row. The director had decided that to denote a scene change the actors would give a short sharp collective clap. At one such 'scene change' my father leapt out of his seat and shouted, "I'm awake!" (At the time it was embarrassing but on the whole his snores were a perfectly reasonable response to the play ...) More often than not, however, my father's presence ensured I was invited into the very heart of the post-show buzz as folk pushed past me to see what he thought – and I began to realise it wasn't only me who enjoyed the opinions of this particular intellectual.

There is a great deal of attention paid to the unfortunate fact that many of our most creative thinkers were/are equally known for their drinking habits. I'm sure there are as many reasons for this as fine single malts to be found in Sandy Bells. In my father's case, he had an earnest need to communicate with actual human beings rather hand down diktats from that proverbial tower. He also knew where he could find the most interesting and vigorous discussions in Edinburgh – in the pubs from the bottom of Leith Walk to the tip of Morningside. It was here that he found a cross-section of our society not afraid of intellectualism but positively embracing it, who think it great crack when one of our clever people eschews the tower and dives into the debate. Of course, Dad's great gift was his ability to express his highly informed thoughts in a manner that was utterly accessible to all. He was as likely to infuse his opinions with sporting analogies as he was to sprinkle them with classical references and he'd assume that his company were *au fait* with both.

I am at present Writer-in-Residence at HMP Glenochil. A job I landed the day before my father died. I wish he were here to enjoy this experience with me. He would have loved to be one of the writers I have invited to talk to the men. He would have enjoyed the fact that they would doubtless have given him a run for his money. He would also have been amused at my shame-faced admission that some men I work with have a better understanding of the classics than I do. It is absurd, really, that my father could feel embarrassed by his education and erudition. Most of us are embarrassed by our lack of it, which is why we enjoy the opportunity to learn from people like him – who are willing to share their knowledge and understanding with *everybody*.

I like to think I have followed my father into the 'family business'. Not show business *per se*, but the business of sharing our rich, cultural history with those who might still perceive it as something only for the privileged few – ie *not* for themselves. I have a playwriting group in the chokey – a group of offenders with a distinctive voice of their own. I have offered them what I know about how drama works, (with a smattering of Aristotle so I don't look like a total eedjit), and they have gifted me their perspective on the world. Because that is something my father taught me: that sharing works both ways and if you engage with people outside of the tower they will teach you something too. I am looking forward to taking the work I have found in Glenochil prison right back into my world. And, given the fear of knowledge that dogs the powers-that-be, I am prepared to smuggle it out if necessary. That, after all, was my father's real business.

We should not eulogise my father's fondness for a drink but we should certainly celebrate his enthusiasm for smuggling knowledge to the people rather than marking it 'Top Secret' and handing it over to the 'educated' elite to use it at will. That mattered. He taught me that matters – and that you can have a truly stimulating intellectual discussion just about anywhere if you just look for the right people rather than the obvious ones.

So for the good of our nation's cultural health, if not for its livers, I hope there is another Angus Calder out there – I'd like to meet him and, yes, buy him a pint.

The Mantle of Time
Bill Dunlop

Death rarely has perfect timing. Some six months after Angus's passing, his absence still seems temporary, as if he has retired to consider arguments about Scotland, Europe, the world and the universe – and will shortly produce a response. Meanwhile, the 40th anniversary of the first photographs of the earth from the moon forcefully remind us how fragile and fleeting our "bonnie broukit bairn" really is.

This particular argument for 'Why Angus Matters' claims his consideration as a pioneering historian with very personal and pertinent views, whose reputation deserves to increase the more interesting the times we live in become. To assever that Angus was a one-off is to diminish our own unique and irreplaceable individuality, a mistake Angus was careful to avoid – perhaps one aspect of his character which made him the kind of historian he was. For someone of his generation and background, educated when and where he was, it's not surprising that he belonged to a British Marxist tradition upheld by the likes of C L R James and E P Thompson. The influence of this tradition is obvious in *The People's War* (1969) and is evident years later in his groundbreaking *The Myth of the Blitz* (1990). Its title possibly misleads. Angus would have happily challenged assumptions that people were homogenous in their stolidly resolute response to the threat of invasion and the reality of bombs falling in their streets and on their houses. This examination of "the myths we live by" is a fine example of what 'revisionist history' can and should mean, and remains one of the most interesting and readable to date.

Having been bombed in his own home, it's perhaps no surprise Angus should take on the task of asking not why it happened, but what was created amid the ruins. Considering film, novels and other media and the ways in which material produced came to serve the greater story which had brought them into existence, *The Myth of the Blitz* is remarkable and almost unique among histories of the period. His agenda was not to provide an alternative narrative, but to illustrate how sense is made of experience from available material, as well as how 'experience' is offered second-hand, through film, fiction and other media, to the point it becomes privileged over lived experience.

It's difficult to judge what will stand up to later considerations. *The People's War*, though out of print, remains an epitomé of British civilian experience during World War Two, only partially replaced by later work drawing on largely the same sources. *Revolutionary Empire* was initially projected as the first of a three volume history of the British Empire, achieved by later writers but from other perspectives. *The Myth of the Blitz*, however, offers a virtually unique analysis of civilian response, partly suggested in *The People's War* but only fully realised in this later work. What is important to remember, however, is the focus in Angus's work on the personal.

It takes us, perhaps, to the heart of the contradiction both in Angus Calder, person, and Angus Calder, historian. For Angus, although the personal was always deeply and necessarily political, he also more than recognised that the reverse was also the case. Angus took E P Thompson's manifesto, to "rescue [the subjects of his study] from the enormous condescension of posterity" and ran with that ringing challenge in his own particular way. There have been more distinguished careers, greater outputs and more noticed historians than Angus Calder, but fewer who have attempted to give due place to the personal and the political with as much conscientious sincerity and insight.

Does this matter? Given the way we live now, encouraged by short-term opportunisms into a form of historical and cultural amnesia, the answer may be; more than it deserves to be in an economically, environmentally and socially challenged world, 'Yes'. Because of 'Us'. The 'Us' that Angus always insisted on being, drunk or sober, past, present and in the future as he had the courage to imagine it, and believed it could be). The enigma wrapped in the conundrum which is human experience and response remains the kernel of historical interpretation and the opening of it to public gaze makes for a process of considerable complexity. Simplifying it offers deeply individual experience up to "the enormous condescension of posterity". As history teaching in Scottish schools becomes a trawl through 'People and Places', pleas for 'relevance' disguise attempts to replace serious study with temporarily fashionable 'skill sets' and Research Assessment Exercises camouflage bureaucratic influence, alternatives become vital. For all of these reasons, and for all of us, *The Myth of the Blitz* has much to offer both in purpose and method. Angus argued that history mattered because to understand it was to understand our selves. For that reason alone, never mind the many possible 'others', he continues to matter to us all.

Muted Brilliance, Froward Pips

Tessa Ransford

Angus Calder was at heart a poet. He won an Eric Gregory Award, the prestigious awards for poets under thirty. Academic life led him into History and to teaching contemporary poetry through the Open University, in which he included Scottish poetry. Angus cared deeply about Scottish culture.

In *Lines Review* 111, 1989, I published a poem of Angus's: 'Soft Fruit above Forfar' which ends with the line "muted brilliance, froward pips". The poem is sparse in words but rich in vocabulary, simple yet profound: "the oats have crisped/ to a susurration and "scry it against/ the whelming Grampians".

Angus's eagerness, expertise and enthusiasm as first Convener of the Scottish Poetry Library were vital ingredients in the success of the struggle to turn that idea into a reality. He brought academic standing to our cause and a wonderful 'can-do' attitude. He was always kind and supportive to me, but also initiated me into an analysis of the socio-historical scene we were living through (Thatcher's 80s). To be in Angus's company was to gain enlightenment, to learn something you didn't know before. Sometimes I thought he was wrong, but he would enter into discussion without disrespect. He was angry with me when I said in an interview once, "Poetry is taboo in the universities". "Of course it isn't", he said. "But Angus, do you talk about your own poetry in university circles?" I asked. "Of course not", he said. Angus continued to support the SPL long after stepping down in 1988, and could be counted on to speak on its behalf and include it in his varied writings about the state of the culture.

When I retired from my work as director of SPL at the end of 1999, and when my husband, Callum Macdonald died earlier that year, Angus was a friend who cared, sympathised, praised and supported. He hugely respected the work Callum had done in publishing and supporting poets. He didn't hold back from saying so, even if it wasn't fashionable in the new millennium to care about anything in the literary scene other than the 'marketable'.

It was sad to see Angus gradually lose his hold on daily life. I was not one of those who 'rallied round'. I reckoned I couldn't add to what others were doing and had enough to do to keep myself positive and productive and support my daughters with their young children. Angus, however, included me in those he phoned in the middle of night with a new poem just written, wanting to read it out and get a response. I know the impulse only too well. It is like a hen laying an egg: "Look, look, look what I've done!" as my mother – a poultry expert – interpreted their clucking. Angus, uninhibited through alcohol, did what we would all like to do after completing the first draft of a new poem. SPL was designed to be a place where poets could 'cluck' and not feel inhibited to talk about their own work, rather than commenting acerbically about the work of contemporaries, or devotedly about the work of the dead.

In 2000 James Robertson's Kettillonia pamphlet press published Angus's poem sequence *Horace in Tollcross, eftir some Odes of Q H Flaccus.* The poems are superb, and only someone with Angus's mix of classical expertise and street-wise experience could have produced them. Each one is a masterpiece. The transformation of Horace's satire on himself and contemporary life is trans-formed hilariously and hard-hittingly into Tollcross, Edinburgh, Scotland, UK, at the turn of the millennium. "Our Muse/ won't let merit perish and can make/ wee nutters immortal. (4.8. page 27 *Donarem pateras grataque commodus*).

Thinking of Angus and this brilliant book, I wonder why we don't have a regular poetry programme on Radio Scotland. Will it happen now? Will the new Creative Scotland give a toss about the wee nutters writing immortal verse under its feet and outwith its controlling beneficence? "… we've/ for-gotten the authors' names but never the words" (4.9. page 29 *Ne forte credas interitura*) is something we could all take to heart. It is what we write that mat-ters, not how many people know that we wrote it or thank us or pay us for it.

In a review of James Greene's book of poems, *A Sad Paradise*, in *Lines Review* 115 1990, Angus writes "This collection provides many pleasures: such as come from deftly managed cadences, witty figures of speech, surprising ideas." Angus himself was the master of all these in his writing and in his life itself. I would add that woven into his self-destructiveness was a wealth of kindness and compassion. From Mowlana Jalaluddin Rumi's 'The Drunk-ards' (translated by Robert Bly) come these lines: "They come with gold sewn into their clothes/ sewn in for those who have none."

"The man's the gowd for a' that" and if we *believe* it, rather than pay lip-serv-ice to it, we know that every writer has unique gifts to offer. The tragedy is that, over the 20th century in Scotland at least, the strong link between writers and the community has been severed. Angus is important because he knew it is a vital link, vital for the writer and for the community. Putting it back arti-ficially is difficult, though attempts are made through residencies. Not many academics and writers of Angus's calibre are prepared to take risks in speaking for the real socio-political, not just literary, need for a Scottish environment to evoke the gifts of multinational writers living in Scotland. Not many writers are content to serve a Scottish public, wanting instead to be known in London and internationally. It is not a case of either/or. The local, if genuine, is also global. The global in itself is bogus. Despite the ups and downs of his private life, Angus was respected locally and globally, without betraying either per-spective. He managed to bring his learning to bear at a political, social and 'street' level, as well as in what David Jones called "the academies". It matters that we become learnèd to the best of our ability, and that we share it and apply it as best we can according to our circumstances. Angus never failed to keep on trying on both these scores and, in so doing, he did indeed succeed.

Alasdair Gray Remembers a Last Visit

I first heard Angus speak in 1982 or 3 when he presented me with the Fred-
erick Niven Award for my novel *Lanark*, and some months later was intro-
duced to him socially by our friend, Peter Gilmour, his colleague in the Open
University. My talk was full of woe for my second novel, *1982 Janine*, then at
a standstill because my Edinburgh publisher could not advance me the £1000
I needed to complete it, and a London literary agency had failed to find an
English publisher who would. Angus suggested I showed the early chapters
to Liz Calder, no relation of his but a director of Jonathan Cape who had
recently published his history book, *Revolutionary Empire*. Liz was a New Zea-
lander, he said, with no prejudice at all against Scottish writers. So I did as he
advised, Liz Calder accepted *Janine* for Cape, advancing me £1000 – worth
nearly £3000 now — so through Angus my best novel got published in 1984.

From then on our paths in the small Scottish literary world kept crossing
and I knew our political opinions were much the same. I was more inclined to
vote Scottish Nationalist than he but we both supported the Scottish Socialist
Party until Tommy Sheridan split it through his court case. By the year 2000
my wife Morag and I were among friends he phoned when he felt like a conversation. These were sometimes longer than we found convenient, though
we liked him too much to end them speedily.

In April 2008 Gideon, Angus's son, asked for a contribution to a book for
his dad, now in an Edinburgh nursing home which he was not expected to
leave. I wanted to contribute a portrait and so visited the home with a sketch
pad. A nurse announced me into a small room where Angus lay in bed, relaxed
and calm, perhaps from morphine, and moving so little that he was easy to
draw. Once I heard him murmur what sounded like an African name, adding,
"A good man." Knowing he had taught in Uganda I said, "Was he a writer or
in politics?" "Politics." Angus had once told me of seeing Idi Amin raised to
his bad eminence by a departing British administration who feared Amin's
black left wing opponents, so I asked how the good man had managed. Angus
murmured, "He had to play with the cards very close to his chest."

I felt that, in general, he was remembering or dreaming about friendly
things. Once, rousing himself slightly, he said, "Where are you from?"

"Riddrie, east Glasgow."

"The near east?"

"No – the east of Glasgow."

"Ah."

I finished the drawing, bade him goodbye and kissed him on the brow.
Without opening his eyes he murmured, "How very kind."

I left after saying insincerely that I would call again soon, and he died a few
days later.

Drawing by Alasdair Gray

Note: a slightly different version of Alasdair's drawing above is the fronticepiece to For Angus, *the volume mentioned in the memoir opposite, which appeared early this year and can be ordered from:* **Jenni Calder, 31 Station Road, South Queensferry, EH30 9HZ – £10.00 inc p&p)**

Why Angus Calder Matters
Marshall Walker

Angus Calder visited the University of Waikato, Hamilton, North Island, New Zealand in December 1995. The magnet was his friend, Alan Riach, and their project to collaborate on a three-volume edition of the hitherto uncollected prose of Hugh MacDiarmid (published by Carcanet in 1996 and 1997 as *The Raucle Tongue*). He sang for his suppers in a keynote speech on 'Poetry, Language and Empire' at the annual conference of the South Pacific Association for Commonwealth Literature and Language Studies.

The discourse engaged by the conference has always been slippery, perhaps more so now than ever. Its very title, 'The Postcolonial Body' – begged questions that underlie the surfaces of history and the literalism, for example, of Leo Kuper's insistence thirty years ago that "dialectic of conflict is always racial". QED South Africa, Rwanda, Yugoslavia, Smith and Mugabe's Zimbabwe and now the tectonic chaos of the Democratic Republic of the Congo – and by 'surfaces' I do not belittle their agonies. A very model of a 'postcolonial body', Angus brought to our antipodal corner all the authority of his *Revolutionary Empire* and the profoundly socialist energy and fierce insight of someone who had been the man, who had suffered with his subjects, who had been there. How good it would have been to hear him speculate about the 'dialectic of racial conflict' that was enacted in the privacy of polling booths in the USA last November, invisible to pollsters, determining the extent to which imperial Republicanism could overpower the appeal of a black presidential candidate defined by tragic, noble Colin Powell as a man endowed with 'intellectual vigour', a 'transformational figure' in American and world politics. There should always be an Angus to talk to about such moments in history.

Of course talking to Angus meant listening to Angus. He held court and, yes, pontificated. Prodigious consumption lubricated but didn't dull. His mind moved at breakneck speed. You got the impression that the booze helped to anaesthetise his impatience with us plodders. You learned not to mind that he hi-jacked any topic you might dare to initiate because what he did with it, weaving filigrees, building ziggurats, was so much richer, more alive, more learnedly cross-referential among politics, history, philosophy and the arts than anything you could have made. So you listened.

But none of us, as Angus knew, is a postcolonial except, perhaps, in body. There's always a coloniser out there with us in mind. Paranoia rules OK and so it should. We may watch the avatars of what we think of as colonialism terminate, fading like final blips of light on the screens of the global village; but the geist, colonialism itself, knows how to go on haunting. As a metaphor, solidly structured by historical fact, colonialism must perennially engage our

attention, surviving as a term in our language of cultural analysis at least as vig-
orously as the concept of the frontier in American history. His grasp of this
gives so much of Angus's writing its motive force. History gives us the exem-
plars and they change, but the condition, even the pre-disposition, remains,
whether we talk of the worldwide American colonisation of cultures and languages, the counter-colonising forces of militant Islam, or the colonisation of
minds by the cynicisms of the media, or the colonisation of academic systems
by administrators and management brutalities to the detriment of 'Man thinking'. In Irvine Welsh's novel, *Marabou Stork Nightmares*, the alliance of colonialism and racial conflict is associated with sodomy and leads to rape.

Would that the academy might be colonised by such as Angus Calder. He
was the real thing, as scholarly as he was restlessly, intellectually impassioned,
one of the truly distinguished historians, literary critics and cultural analysts of
his time. His histories of World War II, *The People's War* and *The Myth of the Blitz*,
have been widely recognized and used as academic texts. His monumental *Revolutionary Empire* won from Edward Said the uncharacteristically gutsy accolade, 'gripping'. He probes his native land in *Revolving Culture: Notes from the
Scottish Republic*, a collection of essays and articles on modern Scottish literature and culture bristling with opinion. This is journalism as art, fast, witty,
penetrating and utterly free of jargon. Angus thinking about our place, sometimes as cheerfully as in his conference message which was, in part, the failure
of English as an instrument of territorial imperialism. The recalcitrant gen-
iuses of Ireland, Scotland and Wales, of a Walcott, an Achebe a Soyinka have
made the language porous with their own idioms, creating many Englishes.
The language of possession became a language possessed. Think how Glasgow has achieved possession in the languages of Tom Leonard and Jim Kelman and how the east coast talks via Irvine Welsh and Duncan McLean.

Given our current global financial crisis, when meltdown can imply the cor-
rosion of national boundaries by the imperative of economic inter-depend-
ence and world-wide monetary co-ordination, what would Angus have
thought about prospects for an independent Scotland in the context of the
North Western European Archipelago? How much of a nationalist was he
really, and how would he have felt about his country today? I like to think a coa-
lition of scepticism and heart might have taken him into the Mexican José
Emilio Pachedo's poem, 'High Treason', as adapted by Alastair Reid:

> I do do not love my country. Its abstract lustre
> is beyond my grasp.
> But (although it sounds bad) I would give my life
> for ten places in it, for certain people,
> seaports, pinewoods, castles,
> a run-down city, gray, grotesque,
> various figures from its history,
> mountains (and three or four rivers).

Bowling Beyond Boundaries
Bashabi Fraser

I had walked from Tollcross to Princes Street. For once the sun was not sulking. The world had gathered in Edinburgh, a rainbow crowd ready to plunge itself into whatever the Fringe had to offer – in August the Festival is palpable. Standing at the Caledonian Hotel, I saw a man teetering on the opposite pavement. I knew that familiar tweed jacket and dark green corduroy trousers. I zigzagged my way through the traffic towards him. One hand gesticulated to me urgently while the other remained firmly in his pocket. "This is outrageous! They are threatening to execute Ken Saro-Wiwa! They can't do that!"

Angus's eyes were screwed up in utter indignation and his nicotine-stained fingers held a forgotten burnt out cigarette. I looked up and saw the banner on St John's Church with Ken Saro-Wiwa's name written boldly on it, defying the casual visitor and the easy banter of a careless populace that skirted our little island of Angus-driven anxiety. This was Autumn 1995. Four months later, Angus's canvassing and pleas, to which many of his friends gave voice, could not stop the military regime from executing Ken Saro-Wiwa with fellow prisoners of conscience in Nigeria. Angus was disconsolate.

His teaching career had taken him to countries in Africa, and for him, his journey into this vast continent was not one into the heart of darkness, but one that resonated with his Scottish Enlightenment ideas, identifying with that igniting spark in people like his poet friend Jack Mapange, who could participate in an international dialogue facilitated by freedom of expression and educational opportunities and choices. I have seen Angus been drawn like a magnet to the only black woman/man in a white gathering, as if answering some inexplicable call from his inner depths to reach out and participate in that 'third space' that Homi Bhabha advocates. So when the G8 were meeting at Gleneagles in 2005, and Scottish PEN decided, since the focus was on clearing African debts, to have a seminar with voices from Europe's neighbouring continent to speak of writing by writers from/in Africa, the obvious choice for the chair was Angus Calder. And he was at the heart of a historic dialogic session, filtering the discussion with his amazing mental agility, aided by his insider-outsider knowledge of the postcolonial writer.

I have seen him crying silently when working on his book on the forgotten Eastern Front in Second World War. The sheer waste of human life appalled him. The freshness of wounds left him drained. We need more Anguses today. Writers and historians who will not turn round and say 'who cares!'

His ill health interrupted but did not stop his books from spilling out and surprising his readers. Whenever he had a new poetry collection, he insisted on not reading alone. He had fellow poets sharing his platform, not willing to be the pole star. And whatever his state, he never failed to turn up at friends' book launches. He was like the indomitable Banquo's ghost, loyal and present when wished for, but not quite finished.

He was not just a writer but a friend of writers. I remember, on one occasion, when the Scottish Poetry Library was crammed with an impossible crowd as there were three book launches happening in one evening, Angus arrived too late to find a seat. He chose the floor with ease and then blissfully spread out his legs and fell asleep and the readings were punctuated by his snores. Mine was the last event. He was up, as if a soft alarm had whispered him awake. He sat up, listened and his clapping was the loudest. It was both embarrassing and moving. But we were grateful for his presence.

If the phone rang in the wee hours and the call was not from India, I knew it was Angus, wide awake, oblivious of the time. He had a poem to read that he had just written. Some of his *Horace in Tollcross* Odes were read to me in sleep-ridden, underwater consciousness, I realised they were brilliant.

He did have some strange tastes. His favourite sandwich was a combination of bacon, pickle, lettuce, chutney, mustard and something else that I have now forgotten. But I forgave Angus for this since he was an unfaltering admirer of my Bengali cooking. However, there were many times when we watched helplessly as his animated conversation filled the room while the good food remained untouched. He was too ill to eat.

I think his food taste was just another facet of his internationalism, which was best reflected in his love of that colonial great game that the decolonised world has unabashedly appropriated – cricket! Books, music, curling, bowling, could wait in the wings while test matches were played out across the world, as Angus sat centre stage in his living room, moaning or exulting as his favourite batsmen missed/made a century or a dependable bowler failed to topple/toppled a star out of the match! This was another topic (and there were many with Angus) on which we spoke the same language as we both loved the 'little man of India' – Sunil Gavaskar – and cheered at every new score from Tendulkar. Angus did not have to work hard at being politically correct. It was his second language learnt through an innate liberalism.

The Angus I knew was a staunch Labour supporter. It came as a surprise when he told us he had turned his loyalties to the SNP. At that time, I did not take the SNP seriously at all – a group of inconsequential dreamers with no solid offers for Scotland. When Angus said he was backing this party, I began to rethink. Like many a visionary, he was right once again. I saw the incredible happen as the SNP took power on the slimmest possible win. And as every day passes, they talk more and more in a language I understand. Sometimes I wonder: does Angus write some of their speeches? Well, now his hovering spirit will have to dictate the political wisdom he was so noted for, for all of us. I am sure he is enjoying Barack Obama's presidency, wherever he is now.

Angus Calder

In Filmhouse Café-Bar on Lothian Road

1. The beggar's insatiable bonnet
   brims with coins but is never filled.

   It infects youth, the habit
   of telling stories
   brief as a fart,
   long as the winds

   Faces in Filmhouse vary.
   As the building frays
   face will persist

   Two-pees drip into the bonnet.
   Enduring faces are transient
   but stories insist.

2. You stare at the visage
   of opportunity lost –
   ace gunfighter's gone.

   Great romance of your life,
   Lauren Bacall
   now wrinkly dear lady

   Somehow through mountains
   Spartacus stumbled
   into that burnt cottage

   Moment loved best though –
   hitmen failed – flee –
   some like it hot – to flaming Brazil.

3. Trailer –'real street kids
   in the starring roles'
   In the street parking places,
   here, barking faces –
   disabled and hale
   enigmatic and ruined
   fresh lads with their project
   craving for celluloid
   buy baked tatties
   while movies are moving.

   Here it's hard to believe
   that the fine world is finite

4. Evening expires soon
    Glasses are shifted from this table
    Time is called.

    Japanese man, Slovak woman
    hirsute fattie-faces
    merge into midnight.

    Filmhouse survives in its fraying
    Beggars have endured
    the chilly mist

    Doors reopen tomorrow
    Here and everywhere elsewhere
    stellar stories persist

On the Death of Virginia Harvie, February 26, 2005

Now that shop assistants smirk at my infirmity
and I can't follow their flip youth argot anyway –
now that a flight of stairs is like climbing Suilven
and only veterans find me at all witty –
I insist on conniving in life because
that budding birch tree shines in March sun
and magpies jaunt in airy branches.
But back from the wedding of an old friend's daughter
your news: Virginia's death.
                    Chris, old comrade,
gabless, I can say little more than I've just written.
Our mortality is not final. Birds nest on.
And in Wales and above the glinting Tweed
old backs will be grateful for her memorial benches,
frail eyes peer keenly for thrushes in the shade.

In K Jackson's Bar

This independent feisty Catalan
asserts her rights against her English teacher.
He's Trinidad by birth, Scots education –
white as the driven coal. Nation of such creatures,
this is our Scotland, come-all-ye country of who got here first
and if you're last, sit-ye-doon Jeannie.
Please test us, and watch Scotland at its worst
ere you give up on us and say we're *fini*.
On Dumfriesshire new-found-muirland
jubilant mongrels dance around the moonlit tomb

of latterly defunct King Charles's Spaniels.
As all we dogs advance to smelly doom
doon, doon that final staircase with no handles
please bear in mind that we're all Catalans
in part, in Dog's eyes, who gives damn few damns,
and don't forget the Latvians of Tobago
while out of distant palms you swallow sago.

In Hock

The day sparkles
like the display of jewellery
in a clean pawnbrokers
where superficially calm customers
attend to admonitions from the assistants
about base metals.

This day's glamour won't last much longer
than raindrops which glitter
on leaves under unexpected January sun –

though the bushes, of course, are ever-
green and we know, right
or wrong, that sun will return
after gales and snow
with spring petals

Polaroid

While mother polar bears explore the ice
lean caribou are crossing miles of tundra –

steal from you, Louis, but it won't suffice.
We hobble to some barren new-found-land

My veteran petulance I'd have you know.
While fagends drizzle in the windy streets

the ghosties of my mother's summer socks
become mere rabbits in a puppet show

In Churchill, Manitoba
where the early polars play
the leaves will get rewritten
a year next Saturday
but squat Orcadian factors
sail no more into the Bay

Note: In 'Polaroid' the reference may be to MacNeice and Auden's's *Letters from Iceland* (1937)

The High Frontier
Christopher Harvie

The worst of times, perhaps?

Angus Calder had been helping us – the Lothian Labour Yes Campaign – to run voters to the referendum poll on 1 March 1979, and we fetched up in Ruskin House, then the centre of the Edinburgh left, and went on to a pub in Leith Walk. The campaign had been chaotic and most Labour folk, with a desperate General Election in view, indifferent. A favourable-ish exit poll had come over the TV. "I have the feeling that this might be our 1945." Angus, pint in hand, fag in mouth, was rare in his elation. The next morning, the reality would be grim ...

Six years later, in the grounds of Edinburgh University's Newington Halls of Residence, (now chic apartments) Angus and Allan Macartney had cobbled together a conference on self-determination in the Commonwealth in the shadow of the Robert Maxwell-promoted Commonwealth Games. "We are still here!" was the message, punched home by Neil MacCormick, circling the place with his pipes, and impressing Ali Mazrui, that year's Reith lecturer. And we were here: the Scottish Poetry Library was going ahead, to do for the nation what Gwynfor Evans' Gandhian campaign for the Welsh-language TV Channel was doing for the much more severely damaged cause of Welsh autonomy.

The best of times

That the bracketing quotes are from Dickens' Tale of Two Cities, his 'take' on Carlyle's French Revolution, seems on reflection characteristic of Angus's literary domain: grand, contentious and Victorian in scale. Angus in the intervening period had been a literary laird at Philpstoun House, not all that far from Stevenson's 'House of Shaws', and into a period of home-brewing. Drink was a continuous theme, ultimately tragic, but as insistent as his beloved Horace's *Nunc is bibendum, nunc pede libero, pulsanda tellus* ... "Now let's drink, and beat the ground with our dancing feet."

In this he was, in Nietzsche's register, both Dyonisiac and Appollonian, which was – for an otherwise douce body – a dangerous place to be, though he lasted longer than Nietzsche, dead at 56. The third element, marked by Dickens, a continuing enthusiasm (Orwell's "generously angry" got not just Dickens, but Angus to a 'T'), was his life in the British literary-media scene in an adventurous and experimental period. 'Metrolit', with its agents and PR-people and accountants, had not yet taken over, and experimentation could be backed. Raymond Williams was a television regular, E P Thompson active in the anti-nuclear cause, John McGrath, Trevor Griffiths and Denis Potter were in full flood. Compare with the present: a culture Skyed, Turnered,

Bookered and Waterstoned out of its skull.

Angus was ambitious and, like me, footloose, The Dominies – his father, Ritchie Calder, father-in-law David Daiches – always at his elbow. I remember a couple of conversations. Ritchie had once told Angus about the outbreak of World War I in his native Forfar. He saw the men march off in August to the station – "And they never came back." "Were they killed?" "No, they just didn't come back." The war had sprung the trap of small-town Scotland, of Douglas Brown's Barbie and Grassic Gibbon's Segget. Both Ritchie and David spent most of their lives away, and Angus accepted there were metropolitan/ cosmopolitan advantages, at least in that fricative period before 'culture' became a market-driven industry. About the same time he compared Allan Massie and Clive James (his seniors at Cambridge). "The difference isn't talent but position." That was in the 1980s. Massie the Scots Tory has worn better, and in fact evolved towards Angus's position. But once the Dominie's away, with his boring canons and epiphanies, playing the game of post-modern irony with the celebs is made for every Norf London teenager …

Angus's ambition was as vast as MacDiarmid's or Carlyle's, but it was orthodox in its fastidious scholarship – not poetic-piratical, manière de Brownsbank or Ecclefechan. To 20th-century British history, the European novel, African literature (where his activism protected the likes of Ngugi and Mapanje), his own poetry, and contemporary Scotland as activist and commentator, he added in the late 1970s the huge task of *Revolutionary Empire*, its first and only volume published in 1981. This was simply too much: like the young farmer in Chekhov's Ivanov who hoists a huge load for a bet and collapses, destroyed by a challenge too far.

Angus's British Empire was unlike any previous empires stemming from folk-migrations or drastic technical or strategic innovations – Moslems and thoroughbred horses, Viking galleys. It was dialectical, as it coincided with capitalist pluralism and capitalist printing, and the dialectic was there in the culture, to be decoded, and on both sides of the business. To get as far as 1783 was remarkable. But thereafter? "Read and read until you can hear people talking": G M Young's injunction would have had to work overtime in such circumstances, running from Macaulay and Rammohun Roy to Hobson and Lenin, Buchan and Nehru. Such progress would probably have required a Craigenputtoch: exile, silence and cunning from a convivial, affectionate man. Improbable in the circumstances, personal and political, of the 1980s.

Instead, he took on a kind of ringmaster role in others' successes: Angus as the Georg Brandes or Goncourt of the literary revival in that decade – *Cencrastus* and *Chapman*, Alasdair Gray, James Kelman, Douglas Dunn – imaginative in itself but whose political engagement provided the basis of the 'Tory-free Scotland' campaign of 1987 and the Convention the following year.

At the same time, the absent torso of the great work, like Ozymandias's statue in the Shelley's poem, must have nagged. There was, even in Angus's last days, high seriousness; on his deathbed, he came to and rounded on MacNeice's 'Spain': "I don't like MacNeice in that flippant mood!" I tried Arthur Hugh Clough's *Amours de Voyage* on the 1848 revolutions: surely we had to accept that we were tourists in others' troubles? "No."

Could this be sustained in the turmoil of the literary city? Or in regular commuting between Edinburgh and the Open University's Walton Hall on the notoriously convivial saloon of the sleeper in the days of John Smith and Martin O'Neill? The remarkable thing was the high standard Angus continued to achieve as a feuilletonist [guerrilla freelance journalist!] and poet, such as his introduction to the first collection of the work of Hamish Henderson, *Alias McAlias* (1992). There he talked of a session with Hamish, folksingers and a good-looking girl no-one had seen before or since as "some meeting on a high frontier of talk" at which the gates always remained open on spectacles ranging from classical Greece to Mandela on Robben Island.

His poetry, sharp, well-observed, and often deeply moving, satirised and consoled: a counterpart to the compelled tone of Brahms's late piano pieces and songs. Memories of the epitaph he wrote when my wife Virginia died produced my contribution to the memorial volume, *For Angus*, 'A bard at Corinth' which wrote itself in ten minutes: the first poem I've written for nearly fifty years, and likely the last.

The stress had proved too much and his health had collapsed completely.

Angus's last days were passed in the Elsie Inglis Nursing Home. Like Scott's Chrystal Croftangry in the Chronicles of the Canongate, 1827, he was an 'Abbey Laird' in the shadow of Palace and Parliament. The bankrupt Croftangry returned to an autumnal industrialised Scotland described – according to John Buchan – with the precision of Turgenev. Outside Angus's 'Croftand-Righ' waited not creditors but death. Only a month later there died Nuala O'Faolain, another veteran of the Open University and Arnold Kettle's 'Modern Novel' course team. Refusing treatment for her cancer – like Angus's, lung cancer and brain tumour – she went out with style, broadcasts on RTE, editorials in the papers, etc. Angus's exit was more traumatic.

Revisited, Angus's poetry shows not just the concentrated compensation of an intelligence denied the long-distance stamina needed for book-writing. The effect was elegiac but also registered a work completed. In 'Anent the Referendum: for Hamish Henderson', written in 1997 (*Colours of Grief*, Shoestring Press, 2002), there are echoes of Yeats's penultimate poem 'Cuchulain Comforted', which Conor Cruise O'Brien called his settling of accounts with the political: "They sang, but had nor human tunes nor words,/ Though all was done in common as before;/ They had changed their throats and had the throats of birds."

In an Edinburgh heavy with MacNeice's "factitious popular front in booze" but thinner than ever in the 'raucle voice' of the pubs, democracy for better or worse had taken over, leading to an unknown new land and, at last, a common journey. The poem, dedicated to one of Angus's great heroes, ends:

> It was as if the forests where kings hunted
> still stood on the Boroughmuir, by the Water of Leith
> and after dark a silent army had massed,
> befriending the gypsies, succouring those people plague
> and leprosy had driven furth of the walls,
> then, in the small hours: moved –
> to reoccupy the Old Town by vanishing
> into its stones, giving each a radiance
> as dawn leapt from the grey North Sea
> over a city where ghosts had reclaimed their own
> flowed in and out of each other and made peace
> to match the quietness of those
> who had strolled to vote, minds made up, gone home
> to sleep as determination was uttered
> and the army of ancestors settled in
> insouciant of approaching winter
> and whispering each to each other about spring.

Eric Wishart, Joy Hendry, Tessa Ransford and Angus Calder after singing Hamish Henderson's much-loved anthem 'The Freedom-Come-All-Ye' at the unveiling of the portrait of Tessa by Joyce Gunn Cairns in the Scottish Poetry Library, 28 February, 2004 – photograph courtesy of Roddy Simpson

The Drunkenness of Things Being Various
George Gunn

Some people take a lifetime to die, fading out of existence like an over-exposed photograph. But with those who fall off the end of their lives, who is to know whether they jumped or were pushed? Then there are those to whom the end comes by accident. Some – too many – go too soon. Hated people, it seems, live forever. When someone is loved and they die, for whatever reason, the pain is unbearable. The time and manner of their death is always wrong.

So it was with Angus Calder and me. You bastard! I thought when informed of his passing, What in the love of god did you have to go and do that for? All that informed yapping and crack we weren't going to have again – What on earth wir ye thinkin aboot, Angus?

Of course, he would have his mind on other matters, as usual. Then there was his funeral which fell slap bang on the opening of a play – so I couldn't go. Typical. I had even thought of him reviewing it. That was fanciful, considering the state of his health. Then I had the notion that I could review my own production as 'Angus Calder' (he would have seen the mischievous idiocy in that). Also, was I going to have to miss a wake for a man held in a pub he was barred for life from? Now that he was dead he was reinstated. "The drunkenness of things being various", indeed. ['Snow', Louis MacNeice]

What was it about this shy, shabby, drunken, ditsy dreamer that I loved? Some men are frightened of failure in their lives and careers no matter the array of their gifts. Angus inhabited the rough jacket of his eventful career and wore it close to him his entire life so that the material smoked almost to combustion from the deep heat of his talents. Not that Angus gave two hoots for the concept of a 'career'. He was far too curious to stick to the same path for long. There were always other lights to follow, different skies and landscapes he longed to walk under and through. His educational model was forged in 18th century Scotland and his eyes were firmly on the possibility of the imagination's liberation in the 21st. His 'organised chaos' was decidedly Scottish.

This nation is not so grand or populous that it can afford to lose so cheaply the likes of Angus Calder. I'm not going to list his many significant achievements from the publication of his debut, *The People's War*, to his emergence, in his later years, as a fine lyric poet. I want to focus on the man I knew for 25 years and what made him special and why he should be remembered.

Angus's form was the essay. Long or short, it mattered not to him. Rarely has a country had such an eyeballing as that administered to Scotland by Angus Calder. He noticed everything. Was interested in everything. Would go anywhere if he thought he was going to learn something. This was not an academic: this was the son of Ritchie Calder, correspondent extraordinaire; this really was "the chiel amang us takin' notes". Angus was an acquaintance of

Reason but he was blood brother to Passion. He wrote as if his life depended upon it, which of course it did.

The measure of any artist as commentator is how they interpret events as they unfold. With hundreds of dead British service personnel in the combined tragedies of Iraq and Afghanistan, the slow demise of the US Empire and the inevitable, messy collapse of the world's rotten financial system under the weight of the lie of 'free markets' and 'globalisation', where is the precise vision of Angus Calder to be found? Where is the informed and compassionate overview we need to make sense of such momentous events? Where is the wit born from a profound depth of reading which can be harnessed to shed light on such confused and confusing times? Perhaps it died with Angus Calder.

The art of the essayist is deceptive. You cannot merely report and walk away from the subject. You have to report and walk into the story. It is the alchemy of the translator. It is what Orwell may have meant when he wrote of being 'Inside the Whale'. Yet whales have very strong gastric juices and can begin to digest you before you realise it. Perhaps Scotland ate Angus Calder?

Let me explain: despite having lived his formative years in England and educated in her system, Angus Calder was one of the most obviously Scottish intellectuals this small country has produced in recent years. The broad church of his interests, expertise and fields of enquiry stand in sharp contrast to the rather narrowing specialisms favoured by the Oxbridge regime. Angus swam happily in the rich currents of the Scottish Renaissance and yet the cultural dichotomies raging within him were apparent to anyone who knew him. It is equally true that these would cripple him as they have done many others.

That he could be funny and sad, outrageous and pathetic in his cups, he shared with many a drunk. The drinking, towards the end – incessant, debilitating and destructive – was upsetting to all who knew him, but it is also the legacy of alcohol abuse and these unresolved interior tensions. Even then, he could still shed light in dark places. I remember a particularly dull poetry reading at The Ceilidh Place in Ullapool with Angus lying unconscious on the floor with everything happening around him. Suddenly he woke up and in his best clipped RP tones asked of the fooshionless poet droning on, "Is that c**t still going on about birds?" Then the vodka mist reclaimed him. That everyone laughed is probably to our discredit but still a mark of our humanity. Nobody present was indifferent. I could have carted him off to his bed but he looked happy enough where he was. The truth was that Angus was never suited to the world of booze. He didn't have the necessary stamina or body mass to carry it off. I feel it carried him off.

He tackled so much, so many 'various things', that perhaps the drunkenness was necessary. I watched him sink, like an actor rehearsing Hamlet, beneath the enormity of the role. Being 'Scottish' was no lesser a role for Angus. And, somehow, being himself was never enough.

Angus never felt that he was 'properly' Scottish. His class background and education, his voice and accent – even the things he loved such as cricket and rugby (and despite his best efforts he could never convince me of their merits) – all seemed to weigh down upon him. No matter what anyone said to the contrary. But the man I knew was generous, loyal, supportive, engaged and engaging, funny, companionable, hard working and modest. That he was frustrated and frustrating, undervalued, neglected, marginalised, addictive, annoying and argumentative just completed his CV as a human being.

Angus Calder was one of the handful of people who have influenced and helped me along the way. His importance in Scottish cultural terms is that he did that for his country too, and for her people, and he expected no thanks. Which is just as well, for outwith the pages of this magazine, he will get none.

He was my elder brother in the muse and I miss him so dreadfully. But I am lucky. I have the vast acres of Caithness to talk to him in. I have the cliffs and headlands nearby that he loved so much and I walk and think about him there. He is in the Atlantic voice of the north west wind and the effortless soar of the fulmar. He never did apply for that council house in Wick, more's the pity.

Angus in reflective mood …

Why Angus Matters
Alan Riach

When Angus came through the Arrivals doorway at Auckland airport, he looked a wreck. Emaciated, nervous, watchful, desperate for a cigarette. He was glad to see me and we walked outside into high New Zealand summer heat, early in December, 1995. When I asked him about the flight he told me he'd managed to get through from Scotland having left his passport behind.

"How did you get half-way round the world without a passport?" I asked. He was evasive. It turned up in the post before he returned.

He'd arrived on a visiting fellowship to work with me editing Hugh Mac-Diarmid's hitherto uncollected prose. Much of this had been gathered by Glen Murray and myself from the archives of the National Library of Scotland. As General Editor, I wanted to arrange the material and provide a context for it both biographical, putting it in MacDiarmid's story, and cultural, explaining how he published and syndicated the material to as wide a readership as possible. But I also wanted a historical context for it and knew that only Angus could provide this. Of all our historians – and there are some excellent historians in Scotland – for me, Angus was, and remains, absolutely pre-eminent.

My judgement is based on his magnum opus, *Revolutionary Empire: The Rise of the English-Speaking Empires from the Fifteenth Century to the 1780s*. This is one book everyone should read in its entirety. I've heard many speak excited high praise about Edward Said's *Culture and Imperialism*, but Angus's book encompasses everything in Said's and its quality has never been fully recognised. There are three major achievements: he described events, locations, movements, moments, people, in massive intricate complexity in diverse parts of the world in the overarching historical narrative he set out to cover. It stands comparison with the best historical writing from any time. Secondly, he understood how great movements, shared ideals and ideas people get caught in, alter society, the way we behave, so there is attention to the inside – beliefs, spirit, will, intuition, sympathy, the history of ideas – as well as the outside – data, diaries, economic facts, the material conditions of people's lives. Third, and most important, he cared about people at the same time as he cared about great art.

He knew what artistic value is, aesthetic priority, why Scott, Flaubert, Joyce are great, he knew what it is that makes MacDiarmid, Pound, Beckett so in touch with real things. And he never subscribed entirely to the pre-eminence of the aesthetic. He could affirm the value of a string quartet in the context of a world war and not devalue the human cost of either, or the worth of the work of art, the need for all the arts. When I asked him once if the one person without whom the 20th century was unimaginable was Hitler, he thought for a minute, then became passionately, intensely angry. "No," he said. "Because

I care about Stravinsky, I care about Picasso, MacDiarmid, Joyce, Shostako-vich. These are the people who make the 20th century possible to live in."

This was why I asked him to write the historical introductions and bio-graphical notes in the three volumes of *The Raucle Tongue*, MacDiarmid's prose, and he understood what I wanted: a context that would recognise MacDiar-mid's unique worth but that would place it among the lives of the people who lived around him. We did a lot of work that December, but my wife and I had to get him back on track first. Rae fed him good New Zealand fare, healthy meals regularly, and we took him swimming. By the second week he was going to the university pool every weekday morning before work. But he was weak. One Saturday afternoon at the beach, I watched him swim out into the bay and saw the tide take him further, saw him turn and swim back, working hard against the tide to get back in. He'd gone out too far. He knew it. When he staggered up the beach he was winded. I could see that he'd make it back but it was clear that he was taking a risk. We didn't say anything about it.

We were all drinking happily at barbecues, dinners, weekends, but Angus regularly visited the nearby off-licence and bottle of gin appeared in the cup-board, to replace its predecessor. "It isn't furniture," we assured each other. "It's not intended to last." But he was getting through quite a lot. Impressively. One night, at a party, he maintained his part in a complicated conversation about Sibelius, Prokofiev, art and internationalism, while becoming increas-ingly comfortable on the living room carpet, until, apparently comatose but undisturbed by the subsidence of his own consciousness, he continued to smoke cigarettes and drink a whole half-pint tumbler of whisky without dis-turbing anything. It was not done to impress. He was not vain, but vulnerable.

Looking back, it reminds me of student life at Cambridge where many of the rooms in which we were taught resembled the big, comfortable libraries a brotherly father might own, into which you'd be invited to quietly read, talk and learn. Papers, notes, half-finished, half-committed lectures, essays, scrib-bled down and left lying in piles, to be collected one day into the magnum opus, were the context of that world. It was pleasant and seductive. I enjoyed it and left. But Angus had in fact delivered that magnum opus in *Revolutionary Empire*, then again in his histories of the Second World War, and in his books of literary criticism about Russian literature (at the University of Waikato, I taught with a Russian specialist who thought very highly of this aspect of Angus's work). He had actually delivered the goods. He was an incredibly hard worker and these books are lucid, strong and insightful.

He also had worked shoulder-to-shoulder at the University of Nairobi with Ngugi wa Thiong'o – a giant of African literature whose great novel, *Petals of Blood* is a modern classic. Angus edited the *Journal of Commonwealth Literature* and knew more about that subject than anyone I could think of, coming at it from the balance of sympathies described above. Working in New Zealand, these things were very important to me, and exemplary.

I guess at the start I was in awe of him. We'd both been at Cambridge, both were committed intellectually to what Angus called 'the labour movement' as opposed to party politics, and were both dedicated to Scotland. I felt humble: he knew a lot more than I did and his judgements were sound.

I met him again through one of the best publishers I ever knew, Martin Spencer, then in charge of Edinburgh University Press. Martin asked me for the book I'd made of my PhD thesis on MacDiarmid's later poetry, especially *In Memoriam James Joyce*. The book was published as *Hugh MacDiarmid's Epic Poetry* by EUP in 1991. When I submitted it, Martin commissioned three readers' reports. He gave them to me on a Friday, told me not to respond to him till Monday. One said publish immediately. The second said yes, publish, but fix this point, elaborate this reference for a Scottish readership, cut that reference because it's ineffective. The third said don't publish this book at all, ever. Each of these readers identified themselves later. Angus was the second, and the most useful. I met him to talk about his suggestions when in Scotland on a return visit from New Zealand. I went over to Edinburgh for 11 am. He came up the slope at Greyfriars Bobby, emerged around the fence with a hung-over smile and took me straight to a bar and the conversation started.

The next trip was even more tight. Every day in Scotland was an allocated series of hours. I met him in his flat in Edinburgh for breakfast. By the end of it, he'd offered me work in the Open University, just to get me back to the country. On the same trip, I'd run into John McGrath at Euston Station in London and had a coffee with him, during which he suggested I might come back and work with 7:84. But there were things to finish in New Zealand, and when I did come back to Scotland, on January 1st 2001, things had changed.

I stayed with Angus in his flat in Spittal Street while continuing research on MacDiarmid at the National Library, and saw him periodically after coming back to live in Scotland. His first book of poems had appeared, *Waking in Waikato*, a main section of it written in New Zealand and some of the poems dedicated to Rae and me, describing where we lived, our wee boy, the tree we could see from our garden, its roots going down and out to all the world: "as if all our forebears/ rushed back through its branches …" Angus saw it as a metaphor, not for rooted, singular identity, but for connectedness, something that recognised differences and worked with them in a friendly and constructive way. Deep in conversation one night in New Zealand, he'd said something about seeing things in a certain way, "On this side of the Atlantic … "

I looked at him directly and paused the conversation. "What side of the Atlantic is that, Angus?"

When I visited him in the care-home a week before he died he was in a bad way. He smiled at me when I came into his room though, and he said, "Well, what side of the Atlantic are we on now?" I miss him.

Angus Calder – Writer in Residence
Grindles Bookshop, 1990-2003
Sally Evans

Of all the writers who have laid claim to the accolade of writer in residence in our bookshops, Angus Calder's reign was the longest, the most memorable, the most inventive and the most inspired. He would begin tutorials by lying on the floor while reciting a new poem from a crumpled envelope, the ink still wet. His audience would step over him saying, "Morning, Angus" if they knew him, or if it was their first visit, casting enquiring glances, to see where they could enroll.

The poem of the morning once discussed – could it be a sonnet if it had thirteen lines? Must it be one if it had fourteen? – he would proceed to the poet of the day, often his favourites Iain Crichton Smith or Louis MacNeice, and subsequently encourage the discussion to roam over shortleets, review lists, Parliamentary procedures, what was on the radio, and who was going by in the street. (On one occasion a bus-load of Elvis impersonators arrived at the hotel opposite, which left even Angus speechless for a while.)

He encouraged audience participation, and contributed to the self-development of book buyers, glaziers after a night's festivities in the Grassmarket, school pupils looking for deviant parents among the bookshelves, or actors and musicians taking a rest from rehearsals in the nearby Traverse Theatre. These would all experience Angus's responses to preferences for Shakespeare, Burns, Fergusson, Ali Smith, A L Kennedy and Alasdair Gray, authors who counted themselves among his friends. I can just imagine him having an all-night session with Shakespeare, perhaps allowing Will to sleep in his front room after landing in the High Street with a mixed-up theatre company. If, however, his captive hearers approached literature through other interests, be these music, opera, politics, cricket, rugby, or booze, the link would quickly be made to Angus's latest writings, readings, theories and anecdotes, ranging over Commonwealth Fiction, world history, current Scottish poetry and writing, the works of MacCaig, MacLean and Iain Crichton Smith, Victorian women's poetry, how Joy was, how Eric [Wishart] was, where Gowan was, and what George Gunn had said to Hamish Henderson in Sandy Bells on some particular occasion in 1989. Another specialism was Scottish political studies.

After a couple of hours of discussion in which up to thirty people might have taken part, Angus would be offered a coffee break, and would normally adjourn to a local parlour such as the Blue Blazer or Filmhouse Bar. Not once did he complain that the bookshop's liquid refreshment was limited to coffee.

Modern communications occupied Angus greatly, but for the most part he coped without the internet, keeping in his pocket a small notebook containing phone numbers for poets and writers, together with those of most politicians, historians, many musicians, opera singers, actors and directors, journalists, most of his family and many perfectly ordinary people like you and me. You just had to say, Grace Nicholls? Tommy Sheridan? Michael Howard? and provided Angus was satisfied with your reason for wanting to contact such people, the relevant phone number would be read out for transferring to your own little book. This system, of course, was the precursor of Facebook.

For somebody who could lean so heavily on his fellows and expect such a lot of support from them, Angus was never much concerned about himself. He needed food and drink, of course, and he later needed housing (mercifully for us, we were no longer next door by the time that problem became acute) but his real concerns were intellectual. He'd have made a pretty good monk – well, in a mixed-sex monastery.

My father knew Ritchie Calder, and I always felt an inevitability in ending up in close acquaintance with his exasperating son. His blend of intellectual curiosity and gossip was irresistible. He would look at all sides of a question, which led to apparent disloyalty at times, as in his frequent changes of political party, reported by the press with progressively less enthusiasm as time went on. He loved things he did not understand – such as bookselling – as much as things he did. There wasn't anyone else remotely like him, and I could always tell when novelists put even a part of him into their fictional characters.

One of the pleasures of being a bookseller is giving books to friends from time to time, and Angus must have benefited from this, but sad to say the only two titles I remember passing on to him, when he expressed his delight on discovering them in our shop, were a Victorian/Edwardian book called *Famous Dunces,* and a flimsy leaflet on Wartime Lettuce Growing. How very Angus.

Colin Donati

Ways of Looking at it

Which 'beauty' to prefer;
your unflinching courtesy on the wagon,
or unflinching outrage off,

you reciting Iain's 'Deer on the High Hills' entire
at the SPL the year 'just after' his passing
when we are here to hear you read your own,

or six years on Lear's ragings at the storm,
straight Marmeladóvian declamation,
dry ditch-straws in your coat and hair

for real

that last hot August
in the Filmhouse café.

Alan Riach

Orkney Postcards

1. The Gloup

Fifty-minutes snatched from schedules took us to
an openness of sky, sea, out-stretched headlands
and the pleasure of the short walk to the Gloup.
    – "I don't know what road we're on.
    Where would you like to go?" (handing over
    the map) "To the moon!" Of course.
The Gloup was good enough. A tiny silver burn
streams down the pathside, suddenly becomes
a fall beneath our feet, the wooden platform
inches from the great stone gulf there, opening
before us: the sea reaching in, reaching up
the walls of stone through a gap in the cliffs,
tidal, remindingly recurrent, the great big tug –
the world is out there, and there's this:
a moment's friendly sense that's shared,
about what's vulnerable, worth keeping hold of
    – opening out.

2. At Eric Linklater's Grave

At Merkister Hotel, on Harray Loch, the water's lively,
blustery wind streams through across the carpark. "Up the hill,"
the hotel owner tells me, "that's St Michael's Kirk.
That's where he's buried. Marjorie too, beside him.
You'll find them: they're there like standing stones."
Sure enough, on the crest of the wind-blasted hill,
my hair and jacket and trousers flapping like flags,
and all the blue bays and green fields before me,
that's where they are. A ragged stone for him, a finger pointing up.
A diagonal line for her, leaning sharply towards him.
"Praise be to God" beneath his name. A little way off,
I see an apple on the grass, one of those you find
painted bright red, for show in shop windows. This one's white,
the bright enamel all washed off. I pick it up, remembering
the words in *Magnus Merriman* (who else wrote like this?):
"Her bra lay on the carpet like two discarded grapeskins."
And I settle the styrofoam apple by his headstone, out of the wind,
and breathe, "Praise be to Him indeed, but give the Devil his due."

3. *Wyre and the Bu*

"Out of this desolation we were born …"
But that was Edwin Muir and clapping psalms
that shivered out the ebb-tide far too far
till nothing seemed returning but a dream of sunny holms,
of fabled horses and – a childhood full of summer.
Today the wind is flattening, the paths' mud
ankle-deep, the fences barbed or wired with shock
for straying sheep or cattle, Muir's father's farm
cold grey in early February light, the road
a running line on time, affording views of islands levelled,
all heights bent down and polished to
their lowly curves and pieties; the wreckage
of a vision, both lovely and unreal.
Returning to the ferry, *Eynhallow*, I'm caught by a man
on the skyline: his cap secure, his shoulders square,
his jacket blown out against clouds.
He's moving, steady, out across the daybreak,
scattering seed. I look again: There are the planted rows.
There is a crop. The muddy water squelches through
my shoes and socks. I walk and clench my toes.

4. *Threaded on Time*

Driving after dark through Hamnavoe at a snail's pace,
manoeuvring the narrow winding main street, past empty
close-mouths, alleyways, voes running down to the sea
where the sea's running up: this tidal little town, on waterfront
and hillslope, steep thin streams murmuring descent.
Ferry, ocean, travellers, return upon their different tides and seasons.
And I. 1976: That long summer's exploration landed me,
one afternoon, with GMB, after a flurry of letters,
this long conversation, as the gift of a salmon arrived,
and knowledge of the hesitancy needed in this given world,
added to by his kind words, supporting. Then 1995:
and me a married man, and GMB again that afternoon,
slowly recollecting, piece by piece: "That salmon, yes,
and you were here with someone, then … But now I'm fallen
'into the sere and yellow'…" Now, 2007: a blue plaque
on the wall. That's good. And on a sunny, windswept afternoon,
there's Warbeth spread before me like a harbour or a comfy bed
new-made. Beside his Mum and Dad, but with the adult words he made
around his stone: a silence to be content in. The salt is in the air.

5. Drawn back by Magic

Whatever the hand holds: camera, paintbrush, pencil, pen,
the fingertips upon the laptop's keys, the paper, screen or canvas
and the air the senses carry in – make traces, tracks, a patterning
that moves out from the place and its location on the clock,
to be caught, glimpsed, held on, whatever may be,
and at whatever time, but never trapped. That is what work we do,
what help it might be, crosses then to now;
but it is not only that. It also brings you back. Something unplanned,
intuitive, relaxed, working in the bones and muscle,
way below the memory of things: abstraction, yet as real
as that salt spray that hit you like a shower switched on
when the ferry smashed the cross-wave and a blast
of blue and green turned white as frost and drenched
you in a sudden cold – as if all resolution, steel and ice
were sensitised. Or that moment in Kirkwall Cathedral,
writing in the book: the third time now, to see in Orkney,
what has changed and what remains, and by whatever
chance and will should be, what's drawn back by magic.

On the Malvern Hills

And the sky's breath lifted both of them,
the blue, the red, two men in harness, strapped
and corded to their pelmets as the air curved them out,
shields in the azure, quilted with this
substantial occupation: the rising thermal currents
making movement of them, human points
and mechanisms, the sounds as unheard
as the streams appeared invisible, in air.

Like reeds, lifted by the wind, over salt hay
by the river's side, loosened and taken,
spiralled by the rising breath and turned
in lengthening loops and figures, arabesques,
the strain borne even by the hands upon the cords,
the pressures bringing down or over,
out, away to one side or high above
the steeply sloping hillsides, the curving downs below.

On the ridge of the Malvern Hills, David runs ahead,
his seven years of appetite lead quickly to the hill beyond.
Our walking's easy, the pace in the heat of the summery day
unhurried. We crest the second summit, see David now
a tiny figure standing on the third, shoulders and arms turned back to us
and then – the paragliders cresting the horizon, sweeping up above him,
sliding down the currents of the col, close to his small shape.

He's looking up at them as they glide by. His breath's intake
I can feel from here – a child whose arms upstretch
to the full moon in the ancient sky, so full of natural want,
for the unattainable.
     – *Windflower*, Elgar called her.
Ah, those rosebud lips. And things all "wild & headstrong" –
"dreaming of a greatness … by the sedge reeds by the riverside."
Looking back at the hill-fort of Caractacus, his little army always
facing impossible odds, but standing even now
unchanged on this "illimitable plain"…
For all the empires of the world have risen to be washed away,
in light-like movement, solid, weighty in the drift of its proximity
     and David's risen gaze – the unreachable things can be seen
and heard as they move in the air.

Lanarkshire, January

low sun –
          late winter afternoon –
the shadows stroll and stretch themselves across
                         the green fields and the iron earth –
the widescreen light is cold and clarifies on paths white with frost,
all the lengthening day,
          from Loudon Hill to Tinto
from Darvel to Drumclog.

The spires of village churches sharpen themselves.
Branches click like blades or needles in the breeze.

Covenanter land: a hard terrain
of outdoor congregations, sheer
determination, beliefs
you'd stand and die with, live for in
commitment, be determined by.

          The bare trees
strain the sunlight in the sky.

Raskolnikov's Dream

from Crime an Punishment, *1.v by Fyodor Dostoevsky*

set owre by Colin Donati

"Wis that me actually thinkin o gaun up by Razumichin's to spier aboot work, him gettin me teachin or somethin …" Raskolnikov wis stertin to mind, "But whit help could he lend us noo? Pit the case he got me lessons, pit the case he even split his last bawbee for us – if he's got bawbees – and seen me guid to buy masel the butes, redd up some claes for to dae the teachin in … hm … sae, then whit? Whit wid the penny-fee for it be gettin us? Thon widna see to ma needs noo. Truth be telt, it's glaikit, me gaun to Razumichin's …"

The question, whit for gaun noo to Razumichin's, had cowped him mair nor he kent even his ainsel; in his fyke he wis aye howkin for some shrewit sklent to yon, on the face o it, plain simple act.

"Ay rite, wis I really thinkin Razumichin wid sort it aw, Razumichin be the lane answer til it?" he spiered at himsel wi misbelief.

He pondered and rubbed his broo and, queerly, aiblins by chance, efter lang thocht, plaff, awmaist by its lane, intil his heid cam this byous notion.

"Hm … to Razumichin's," he said, perfectly lown suddenly, like wi a sense it finally wis settled. "Ay, for sure, I'll awa to Razumichin's … jist, no the now … I'll awa to his … the day efter; efter *yon,* when it's aw bye and done wi and awthing taks a new turn …"

And syne it hut him.

"Efter *yon!*" he gowled, lowpin up frae the bench. "Is it awa to happen? Could *yon* actually be?"

He quit the bench and wis aff, jist aboot leggin it; he had been for turnin hame, but ony thocht o hame noo wis the fellest o scunners: there, in that neuk, in thon hangished press, for mair nor a month noo, aw *yon* had been maturatin inside him, and sae he jist follaed his een.

His nervish chitters wis turnin feverish; he felt chilled even: sic a heat and he wis cauld gettin. Like wi a strauchle, near kenlessly, as if frae some deep inner need, he goved hard at awthing roond aboot him, as if seekin distraction, but couldna haud at it and aye fell back intil his thochts. Syne, liftin his heid to gawp aroond wi startle, he wid clean forget the thochts and even whit gate he wis gaun. Thus he trailed the breadth o the Vasiljevsky Inch, arrived at the Lesser Neva, crossed owre the brig and turnt his sails for the Isles.

At first the greenery and callerness soothered his trauchled een mair yaised wi the stour and lime o the city, the great muckle thrang tenements. Here wis nae smochiness, nae reek, nae howfs. But it wisna lang or aw thae blithe new sensations wis back to pine and canker. Whiles he wid staun lookin owre some-or-ither brichtly pentit *datcha* set in amang the summer fulyerie, keek in throu the fence and watch, faur awa, the bonnily buskit wemen on the terraces and balconies, the bairns scoorin aboot the gairdens. He got awfie taen up wi flooers; goved langer at thaim nor ocht else. He met in wi grand cairrages, men and wemen on horses forby; wid follae them wi his een and cease to think o them afore they were gane frae his sicht. Ae time he stopped to coont his siller and fund it come til aboot thirty kopecks. "Twinty to yon polis, three to Nastasya for the letter … that means the Marmeladovs yestreen got forty-seevin, mebbe fifty," he thocht, toatin it up, syne forgot for whit he had poued the siller frae his pootch. He minded again as he gaed past this kinna cook-hoose like a licensed pastie-shop and jaloused he wis needin to eat. Ben the shop, he swallied a vodka and taen a bridie wi some-or-ither stappin til it. He feenished this on his road. He hadna had vodka in a lang while and, tho it wis jist the ae gless, it strauchtwey took his heid. His shanks suddenly wis like leid and a stoondin need to sleep cam owre him. Turnin for hame, he won as faur as the Pyetrovsky Inch, deid duin, stopped, left the pad, fell in amang the busses, drapped to the gress and instantly wis owre.

In feverish states, dreams is aften set apairt by their byous veiveness, skyre focus and unco likeness to life. The scenes that unfauld micht weel be ferlies, but aw the kelterin backclaiths and action in them are that leal, wi details sae perjink, sae unexpectit, yet artistically wyce, as pairt o the haill pictur, that the same sleeper waukent could never hae ingyned the feenished spectacle, no gin he were a makar grand as Pushkin or Turgjenev. Sic dreams, sic feverish dreams, are aye lang minded, and leave a deep mairk on the sleeper's jangled and awready sair bruckle corp.

Raskolnikov dreamed an eldritch dream. He dreamed he wis back in his bairnheid, back in his hame toun, seevin year auld and oot wi his faither on a fair's day for a raik aroond the mairches o the toun afore gloamin. A loory, swaltry nicht it is; the kintrae jist the wey he minded it – in fact, mair mirk in his memory nor whit kythes noo in the dream. The toun stauns oot, bare, like on a paum, wi nae birks near; jist the black straik o a shaw at some faur boond o the lift. A step or twa ayont the hinmaist o the toun's kailyairds stauns the howf, the muckle biggin, yin that aye brocht sic feelins o scunner, even dreid, as he cam oot by it on raiks wi his faither. Aye sic a clatter there wis, sic shouts, lauchter and sweerin, sic coorse, unbonny sangs and a bonny nummer o fechts, that mony stoshious and hackit-faced gubs wis aboot the place. On his road by, he wid haud himsel ticht in til his faither and trummle frae tap to fit. The road in by the howf is aw jist stoor and the stoor aye bleck.

This road, a dirt-pad jist, wynds on anither twa-three hunner steps til it hauds richt to skirt roun the toun ceemetry. In the mids o the ceemetry is the stane kirk wi its green cupola where he gaed wi his ma and da twiced a year for mass when the memorial services wis hauden for his grandmither, deid lang syne, that he had never seen. They aye brocht a funeral bannock (*kutya*) rowed in naipkins on a white ashet – a special bannock made wi sugar and rice and steekit wi raisins in the shape o a cross. He luved this kirk wi its auld-far-rant ikons, maistly set withoot frames, and its auld priest wi the nid-noddin heid. In aside his grandmither's lair, merked wi a trochstane, wis the wee, sma graff o his younger brither, deid at sax month auld, that he also never kent and couldna mind on, tho he wis telt he had haen a wee brither, and on veesits to the kirkyaird, ilka time, he wid mimly and reverendly cross himsel owre the graff, boo doun til it and kiss it. And this is whit he dreams:

He's oot wi his faither on the road up to the kirkyaird roond by the howf; he hauds on til his faither's haun and keeks back at the howf wi dreid. This unco scene grups him. It looks like somethin special is awa to happen. In by the howf is a thrang o tounsfolk aw dressed to the nines, peasant wifies and their men, a haill craw's weddin, awbody fou, awbody singing. And in afore the ingang to the howf stauns a cairt. But an awfie strange yin it is – yin o thae great cairts a muckle aiver gets yokit til for to draw guids and gear, stowes o wine casks and the likes. He aye luved to watch thae big cuddies, thick-maned and sture-shankit, movin lown, wi a meisured gait, druggin a haill moontain ahent them wi nae the least puggle, as if the draucht jist made it aw the easier. But noo, a queer thing, yokit til this big muckle cairt is a wee skrank shilpit peasant's mear, yin o a kind – he'd seen it aften – that gets puggled whiles wi jist a high laid o sticks or strae, specially when the draucht gets glaured doon or stickit in a rut and, in their ply, the peasants aye whuppit them, sae sair, sae sair, on the snowt whiles, or even owre the een, and he wid feel that sorry, that sorry watchin it, it wid near gar him greet, sae as his mither wid hae to wyse him frae the windae. But noo, on a sudden, mair o a roar sets up. Frae ben the howf, wi heuchs and sangs and balalaikas, skails this paircel o big-bookit peas-ants in festive sarks o reid and blue wi jaikets flung owre their shooders. "Finn a seat! Awbody, finn a seat!" yin o them bawls oot, aye a laddie yet, wi a stumpy neck and fat, reid-as-a-carrot coupon, "I'm cairryin yese aw! Finn a seat!" But the lauchter and shouts jist gets stertit:

"That auld naig haud draucht!"

"Yae, Mikolka, ye've tint yer harns, yokin yon jaud to sic a laid!"

"Ay brithers, she's twinty if a day!"

"Pile on! I'm takkin yese aw!" cries Mikolka again and, first yin in, lowps up, cleeks haud o the reens and stauns tall at the front. "The steed jist left wi Matvei," he shouts frae the heid o the cairt, "and this beast, brithers, breks ma hert. I'd sooner kill her, she aye jist eats. Pile on, I'm tellin yese. She'll gallop! I'll hae her gaun fu lowp!" And he taks a whup in his haun, awready fidgin at the thocht o layin intae the gry.

"Haw, tak yer seats, eh!" the crowd gollers. "Ye hear? She's gallopin!"

"Never been a lowp or gallop likely this last ten year, that yin!"

"She'll lowp noo!"

"Nae mercy, brithers; find whups, onything! Whit's yer problem!"

"Gaun; up wi yer aixes!"

They aw stert pilin on to Mikolka's cairt wi lauchter, aw makkin baurs. Sax manage on and it aye has room for mair. They haul up a sonsie, reid-faced wumman. She's buskit in reid calico wi a kurch (*kitchka*) on her croon and thick leather butes tae her feet, cracks nuts and is fairly a wife wi a raird. And aw the fowks watchin lauchs tae. Ay, and how could they no – sic a puir wee craitur awa to draw a haill laidit cairt o them, and at fu skelp, tae!

Twa loons in the cairt taks whups for to land Mikolka a haun. The cry comes: *Ca!* And the mear pous wi aw her strenth, but raither as gallopin, canna even shift it; jist sclatches hard wi her shanks, pechin and courin under the clours o three whups hailin doon ontil her back. The lauchs frae ben the cairt gets louder, but Mikolka, fleein wi rage, jist gies it faster licks wi the whup, as if he really thinks the mear is able for to gallop.

"Lat me on, tae, brithers!" shouts anither gadge, aw enthused, amang the rothos.

"Pile on! Awbody, pile on!" cries Mikolka. "She's takkin yese aw. I'll feenish her!" And he lets welp at her, lets welp at her, til he's in sic a birl he haurdly kens whit he's aboot.

"Daddy, daddy," he cries til his faither, "Daddy, whit for are they huttin the puir horsie?"

"Come awa, come awa!" says his faither, "they're fu, they're fuddelt, jist oot on the randan. C'moan, dinna look!" And he's wantin to wyse him awa. But he wins free and, forby himsel wi gast, rins owre to the cuddy. But the puir cuddy is haein a sair time o it. She pechs, stops, gies it mair yerks, is near aboot to drap.

"Hack her doon!" yawls Mikolka, "That's whit it's come til. Intae her!"

"Sae ye're a Christian, na? Ye black deevil, ye!" shouts an auld codger frae amang the thrang.

"Whae's seen the like, a wee sheltie haulin yon," adds anither.

"Ye're killin her!" yollers a third.

"Dinna meddle. It's ma gear. I'll dae whit I like. Pile on, mair o yese! Awbody, pile on! I'll hae her gallopin! …"

Suddenly awthing gets drooned oot in a haill eructioun o heuchs and lauchs. The mear, no able to thole the faster clours, sterts theivelessly to kick. Even the auld man canna help but smile. Really, sic a dwaibly wee craitur and aye kickin! Twa carls frae the thrang gets mair whups and rins up to the mear for to scad her sides. Each taks yin flank.

"On the muzzle! Gie her it owre the een, owre the een!" cries Mikolka.

"A ballad, brithers!" shouts a body frae the cairt, and awbody sets up. A coorse sang dirls oot, shaks o a tambourine, whustles for the chorus.

… He rins up to the cuddy, rins hard up forenenst her, sees her gettin cleeshit owre the een. Gettin it owre the *een!* He greets. His hert is in his mooth, tears trinnlin. Yin o the whup's cleeshers skliffs his face: he disna feel it. Wrythin his hauns and yawlin, he rins up to the hairy-bairdy auld man that shaks his heid and denunces the haill business. A wifie grups his haun and wants to wyse him awa, but he wins free and rins back to the mear. Awready she's doon til her last stech, but again sterts kickin.

"Ech, the deil be in't!" scraichs Mikolka, bleezin wi anger. He flings aside the whup, lowts doon to the flair o the cairt, hauls up a thick, lang cairt-trammle frae the boddom o't, taks a grup o an end o it wi baith hauns and, pugglin, raxes it high abuin the mear.

"Storm's aboot to brak," they aw cry, "He'll fell her!"

"Ma gear!" Mikolka yollers and, giein it fou laldie, brings doon the trammle. Thi'r a deidly thud.

"Hut her! Hut her! Whit for did ye stop?" shouts voices in the crowd.

Mikolka gies the tram anither hyke and a secont blaw whudders doon ful square on the puir cuddie's rigbane. Her hin legs gies wey, but yinst mair she stachers up and yanks forrit, forrit, wi aw the poost she has left, first yin wey, syne tither, ettlin for to haul the cairt, but sax whups scads her frae ilka side and the cairt-tram gets liftit again, syne faws a third time, syne a fowert, wi hivvy, meisured cloors. Mikolka is pure bealin at no fellin her wi the ae dunt.

"She's haudin oot!" comes shouts.

"O, she'll drap. Hasna a chance this time, brithers!" observes yin fanatic.

"Tak an aix to her! That wid end it!" cries a third.

"Aich! Awa an dine on midges! Oot ma road!" Mikolka cries oot in canker, casts awa the tram, lowts deep doon intil the cairt and puls up a steel gellock. "Mind yersels!" he wauls, and wi his haill pouer dings it doon intil the puir cuddie's back. It huts hame. The mear stachers, saigs, had only wantit to haul, but doon dings the gellock yinst mair and she draps to the grund like her fower legs jist falded, instant.

"Mak an end!" scraichs Mikolka and, as if forby himsel, lowps doon frae the cairt. Mair hauf-steamin, reid-faced gangrel laddies clanks haud o whit comes to haun – lingels, pykes, a caber – and rins to the connached mear. Mikolka plants himsel sidelins oan and sterts lounderin brainishly wi the gellock. The mear raxes her muzzle, sechs oot a last braith, and dees.

"Feenished!" cries a voice.

"Whit for did she no gallop, then?"

"Ma gear!" yawls Mikolka, dandlin the gellock in his hauns, een aw bluid-run. It's like he's wae at haein nocht mair to cudgel.

"Ay, no a Christian bane in yer corp, that's nae lee." shouts a bonny nummer o the crowd.

But the puir laddie is by himsel wi grief. Wi lood skirls, he shoos his wey in throu the thrang to the grey mear, thrists his airms roond her deid, bluid-besmottert snowt and kisses it, kisses it on the een, on the lips … Syne, in a gliff, reid wi rage, he's up and at Mikolka, hammerin awa at him wi his wee neives. That meenit his faither, chasin him aw this while, cleeks him up and lifts him awa oot frae the crowd.

"C'moan, c'moan noo!" he's sayin til him. "We're gaun hame."

"Daddie! The puir horsie … whit for did they … dae for her!" he greets wi bursten lungs, but his words are jist like fobs risin frae his ticht breist.

"They're fu! They're fuddelt! It's nane o oor business!" says his faither. He pits his airms roond his faither, but he's aw clochert up, aw clochert up. He wants to draw braith, to yoller oot, and waukens.

He waukent in a swait, his hair aw plottit wi swait, souchin braith, and heezed himsel up in a gast.

"Thank God it wis a dream, jist," he said, sittin himsel doon agin a tree and gowpin for air. "But, whit's happenin? Am I comin doon wi a fever? Whit an ugsome dream!"

His haill corp felt wracked, his sowel daurk and distroubled. He prapped his heid on his hauns, elbucks on knees.

"Goad!" he cried oot, "Is it een possible, een possible I could tak an aix, gie her a wanner on the heid, crack her croon, skite in the warm, claggy bluid … knap the lock, steal and trummle … slype aff in hidlins, aw smoored wi bluid … wi an aix … Lord, is it possible?"

As he said it he wis shakkin like a leaf.

"But whit's wrang wi us?" he continued, sittin up again, as if in deep dum-fooner, "Na, I ken fine I'll never be gaun throu wi it. Sae whit for dae I torture masel the haill time? Even jist yestreen, yestreen whan I wis awa makkin yon … *trial* o it – even yestreen I kent for shair I widna gae throu wi it … Sae whit's aw this aboot noo? Whit am I aye switherin for the haill time? Fact is, yestreen, on the stair, I telt masel it wis fousome, ugsome, vile, vile … Jist the thocht o it had us cowkin, *for real,* and gart me grue …

"Na, I'd never gae throu wi it, never! Even grant, even grant nae douts in the calculations, even grant aw ma conclusions drawn owre this past month staun plain as day, clean as coontin. Lord, even then, I couldna bring masel! I widnae gae throu wi it, I widnae! … Yet even noo, I'm …"

He won back til his feet, glowered dozently aboot, bumbazed at the place he had brocht himsel til, and made tracks for the Tyuchkov Brig. He wis palie, his een wis burnin, and he wis bane-weary in ilka limb, but fund it easier, sud-denly, to breathe. He felt lowsed noo o yon terrible burthen that had lang been prammin doon on him and noo, suddenly, aw at yinst, awthing in his sowel wis saucht and ease. "Lord!" he prayed, "Licht ma road and I'll be done wi yon bedeevilin … dream o mines!"

Andrew C Ferguson

In Greyfriars Churchyard: Still December Day

Psychic investigator,
I step around the statue. Stones march
between the living and the dead
through a gap in Flodden Wall
to the giant's moss-carpeted staircase
of early nineteenth century rows.

Between monuments, another:
a man with shoulder-length grey hair
– tramp or academic – crying?
I take the other avenue, turning now and then
to see if he's still there.

Superlager cans,
blankets, and a bright burst of graffiti
on the stone-bound plots of parents
and their long-dead infant children
intrude in this diachrome of moss and stone.
They run ghost tours here now,
£12 a chill from Bloody Mackenzie's tomb:
why do we haunt this place
when there's living to be done?

Retracing my steps
I see him talking to an invisible someone.
I leave him alone
in this fish-tank of the dead.
Let me surface at the graveyard gates
to treat with the living again, to feel the marrow
in the great stone bones of Edinburgh.

Killer Starling Nightmare

No peck on the neck
from this man-or-woman sized thing,
its oil-green wings a petrol sheen of feathers,
hiding claws.

Then behind it, clutching at its feet,
bumping at its tail,
becomes a girl – responsive.

Still the claws remain despite her willingness;
those nails could rip out my heart
by accident, or design.

I turn my woman-sized starling round,
pulling her close.
The erection unfurls beneath me
sprouting hands, and a tongue.

Written in 1996, after a Dream

Last night I dreamt
that all the many mirrors in New York
and all the reflecting surfaces
broke in a thousand pieces.

Millennia of bad luck
only avoidable, the experts said,
by shipping all the fragments
to the four corners of the earth
they first came from,

to settle somewhere, all-wheres, at last,
like the dust of the ancients
settles on a lamp shade,
or as a butterfly in China
causes floods in Panama.

Then I woke, trying to make sense
of the dream,
but could only imagine the economic viability
of the shipping costs, how the deal stacked up,

as the dust of the ancients shrouded me
and a butterfly breathed on a mirror
somewhere in New York.

Edinburgh/Fife Circle

Skating on clattering iron hooves
the train edges, lurching and braking,
between home town, and home city
loosely lined by rail;

line-builders once blasted Empire
through the yielding Fife countryside,
the coalfields and the jerry-built mining towns,

to factory-sites now buttered yellow-brown
with endless housing.

The railway remains – an old, wood-stitched scar
grown black through the skin of the land.

The Love Song of Doctor Calamari

Shapeless, my patients, despite their stick bodies,
they wheeze and wheeze about their vile disease
– hard-swimming viruses, humping a payload of shame;
I plumb their imaginations, looking for an escape,
a plughole of the psyche I can reach to find my own.

This is a shallow people. There is no way through,
only cold, hard surfaces, minds like steel cages.
I am alone in a world of gaseous uncertainties.
At night I sing of my love, her blotches
blushing blue somewhere in another Earth's ocean.

Unmarked Grave

Panic. Blind panic,
striving to escape this coffin of hot flesh
in the pressing dark

The moment is seized
by the impossibility of future.
Sweat glands of venom smear the space;
fear enshrouds me
shrink-wrap perfect.

We are the Perfecti, entombed
in bone cages, within tissue walls
and a darkness no-one can recall us from.

Death not a death in itself.
Here we go boys – over the top.
Do not go gently …

The *petit-mal* death of knowing death
has a hundred creeping ways,
and a chummy, icy handshake.

There are indeterminate numbers of 3am's
before my soul is set free.
It squawks in the doorway,
afraid of the blankness beyond.

Stephen Nelson

sailor
saviour

sail
or
sink
or
savour
souls at sea

wind wood water matter
wind wood water
wind wood
wi woo wi woo
wi woo

mast matter
wood matter
master
mariner
save our
souls
our
seas
our
souls
or sail
in wind in wood in matter

sinking

sail
or
sin
in waste in water
wood or matter
water's matter
soul's matter

sinking

sailor saviour
clean or calm

the soul
in sinking matter

mast maker
raise
a sail
a soul
assail
in wind on wood in water
raising making masking making

still the sailor
drowning
calms the soul the sun
the sea

wind wood water matter
wind wood water
wind wood
wi woo wi woo
wi woo

drowning
sailor
raised from
water
stills the storm
softens matter
stills
the soul the eye
the sail
in calmer water
wood and wind
in clearer matter

sailor
saviour
sifting
souls
through wind in wood
sifting singing saving singing
sing

our souls
through seas
our souls
through
wind and world
to clearer matter

singer
saviour
sifting souls
sailing sifting singing saving
sail our souls
to worlds of clearer
singing

. . .

the sea: in flavour
forever

the sea in flavour:
forever

the sea forever:
in favour

the sea: forever
in favour

desert
tree

ocean
light

silver
rock

ecstatic

. . .

light

eye

light

e c s t a t i c

the harbour
gulls
a family
picnic,
now as then,

taste and smell
spinning
in a chip shop –

wonderful

futures

in salt air –
over salt fish,

father's

memory,

chip salt
taste
warning
of memories lost,
disrupted

Salvation Inn

John Grace

It was a black day, as always. The rain hammered down on the cars that crouched, steaming and grumbling, at the traffic lights. Long John Silver stepped into the road. The grumble rose to a roar as the massed vehicles leapt forward as one giant beast and screamed off, splintering into jagged red pieces in the filthy mist and spray.

"Damn and blast ye to hell!" he shouted as he flung himself backwards, lost his balance and crashed to the pavement. Captain Flint shot into the air, squawking and spitting feathers. How in black Hades had he fetched up on Leith Walk at the peak of Friday rush hour? Swabs wouldn't be as keen going the other way, he'd lay to that. He clenched his teeth and began the painful, protracted business of hauling himself to his feet with the crudely-hewn crutch, as the parrot settled back on his shoulder. No one stopped to help him up. He stood for a minute, until his harsh breathing slowed to normal, then he lurched off in search of quieter streets, grunting with the effort of each step.

Edinburgh in the first years of the 21st century was not the town it had been when he had known it as a younger man. Everything had changed, every damned thing. Oh, there were still cobbled streets and tall, dark closes from the Lawnmarket to the Canongate and the dark bulk of the castle still loomed over the city, but the Old Town was a tiny speck of familiarity in the vast sea of odd-looking buildings and smooth, black streets that had swallowed it. And what had happened to the Nor Loch? They must have drained it. It was all too tall, too wide, too big – and infernally noisy! Thousands upon thousands of these blasted horseless carriages filled the streets at all hours of day and night. Not that there was much difference between day and night of late; it was always overcast and it hardly ever stopped raining. And – a strange thing – the rain never seemed to disperse the thin mist that blurred the edges of everything. How long had he been here anyway? Decades piled on decades. His early memories were as blurred and elusive as the mist.

Wandering through his thoughts, he didn't pay much attention to where his feet were leading him and he abruptly came to, as always, to find himself standing in front of a massive, weathered oak door, without the least idea of how he had got there. He sighed and scowled and vowed, as usual, to pay attention next time to where he was going. Then he pushed open the door, lurched inside and banged it shut behind him.

The inn was old; no one knew how old. It was not a place you would find easily. Not many even knew it existed. He hobbled over to his usual place by the fire, bellowing at the stooped figure behind the bar.

"Grog, ye son of a whore! Grog, for the love o Satan!" He was freezing cold and his stump hurt like purgatory. He poured the water out of his tricorn hat, eased himself into a chair and let out a long, noisy breath. He fumbled for tobacco and matches and slammed them down on the table. The innkeeper came with the rum. Silver took out a coin and slammed that on the table. The innkeeper took it, put it in the pocket of his apron and shuffled off without a word. He had never spoken a word as long as Silver had known him.

"He been 'ere since I been gone?" the pirate asked of his retreating back. The man half turned and very slowly shook his head. The ageing seaman looked around the familiar room. He knew every beam and panel, he reckoned; every crack and stain and knothole; every soot-blackened stone, and God, he was weary of it! Sometimes he would add gunpowder to the grog, sometimes he'd throw chairs at the rows of bottles, or at the window or on the fire to ease the tedium, the strain of the endless waiting for a man who never came. But come he would. Come he must. Someday. Silver was sure of that. He lit his pipe and sucked the smoke deep into his lungs.

A mist swirled outside the windows; the daylight was almost gone. You couldn't see the sea but could feel it out there all the same, sullen and alien and huge. As the heat from the blaze and the rum seeped into his bones and the steam rose from his sodden clothes, his muscles began to unclench and he slumped further down into his chair. He looked around. Nobody. He was always the first in. Wilfred would be next, then John and Tam, all of a lump. These were the old timers, the ones he loved and hated and fought with. There were others that came and went, but they were peripheral, anonymous: he didn't have much truck with them. All of them waited for someone.

The door flew open and hit the wall with a bang like a thunderclap. A tall figure strode into the room, cloak billowing. The figure removed the cloak with a flourish and threw it at the landlord. Silver winced. Every night. Every blasted night this performance. Why in black hell couldn't he just slip the thing off and lay it over the back of a chair? Did he still think he was living in his blasted book? The newcomer stalked across the room and sat down, scowling, on a bench in the corner. The water ran off his boots and scabbard and pooled on the slabs of the stone floor.

"By my troth, this sodden land is become very hell, when the crazed hordes do scream about in their stinking machines and render foul God's sweet air. How long must we linger here? Eftsoons I shall be mad as they. Innkeeper! Wine!" He remembered himself and softened his tone: "If you please." He shook his grey, leonine head, spraying water like a dog, then turned and nodded at the pirate.

"What ails ye, Wilfred, this fine evening?"

"I'd as lief be back in the blazing Syrian desert, fighting the infidel, as lie longer in this drenched and sorry kingdom of fools." He turned away, muttering into his beard. Silver shrugged and burped. He could usually get a rise out of the knight, but he sensed the man was depressed and would not afford much sport tonight.

The innkeeper had hung up Sir Wilfred's cloak and was about to shut the door, when two more figures squelched in out of the black night and stood dripping on the flagstones.

"John! Tam! A pleasant surprise and no mistake," said Silver, flinging wide his arms, but not getting out of his chair. "Come join me in a little libation an' tell me what you be doin' abroad on a night the like o' this."

The two sat down at the massive oak table that stood in the middle of the room, silent as dead men. They had long ago stopped responding to his ritual utterance. They were always there, all of them. Always at the same time of night, every night and all night long. Always they waited, each for his master. Always it was the same – nobody came.

Something was different, though, Silver thought. Tonight, something was different. Everybody was morose, preoccupied and it wasn't the weather; it wasn't the endless waiting. Something else. Something new.

The silent innkeeper drifted about, lighting the lamps and candles. Shadows loomed on the walls. This inn, thought the old buccaneer, had lived too long. The smells of ten thousand years of smoke and wine and oil and scent; of sex and sweat and leather; of horses and boiled meat and candle fat hung about the stone walls and the blackened beams like a shroud. An unseen clock ticked ponderously. The tired ceiling sagged, as though it would fain crash to the floor in decent ruin and let time wash away the remains with cleansing wind and rain. It wasn't just the inn: they had *all* lived too long. If only the bloody man would come!

One of the figures hunched at the table slowly raised its head. The face was thin and chalk-white under the tammy, the eyes shadowed into sockets in the flickering lamplight. The thin, wide mouth split itself into a black gash.

"The mooth o hell!" it said. "Sichts nae man could behauld and stey sane – that's whit Rab gied me tae shoother at Alloway Kirk that cursed nicht. I see them yet. I see them yet ... ! But I maun bide. I maun bide til he comes." The speaker lifted an unsteady hand and snatched off his bonnet. The skull rose like a mushroom out of the few wisps of encircling white hair. Silver had heard all this a thousand times.

"Belay your Scotch gibberish and speak the King's English ye bleatin' little bugger! There ain't a man 'ere but 'as the same boat to row and you can lay to that. Stevenson did as bad for me. Took off my good leg with a stroke o' 'is pen and nary a backward glance. Aye! Turned the world agin me an' 'adn't the decency to kill me outright. No matter to 'im what become o' me arter 'e'd finished 'is little tale."

"Ah but he didnae mak a fule o ye," hissed Tam. "He didnae hae the hale warld lauchin at ye the while ye were gaun aff yer heid wi the sicht o that hellish crew and that ... *rattlin* soond ye cannae ever get oot yer ears!" His voice rose to a shout and his companion laid a restraining hand on his bony shoulder.

"Steady on old chap, there's no need to er ... landlord, could we have two large whiskies please. Soon have you sorted out old chap, soon have you sorted out." He made as if to pat Tam's arm and then changed his mind. His hand hovered in mid air for a second, then was slowly lowered and slipped into a trouser pocket. Silver hawked and spat into the fire. A green gobbet sizzled briefly on a glowing log. He scratched his groin luxuriously.

"By the powers, Doc, you got a lot to learn an' no mistake. Old Arthur's made a right fool o' ye. An' 'e only done it so that brainy-britches detective could shine at the side o' ye. That be clear as daylight to a bilge rat."

"Come now, Silver, I'll hear nothing against Holmes, he ..."

"Now, I ain't sayin' nothin' agin your honoured colleague, John; what I *am* sayin' is that you ain't the dunder'ead you *thinks* you are. That's the way you was wrote but that ent all there is to ye, not by a long sea mile it ent. Ye're still bustin' your britches tryin' to be like he wants ye to be, only it don't do no more. It don't do." He frowned and stuffed more tobacco into his pipe.

"I served on the North-West frontier you know," Watson said, after a long silence. His gaze was distant. "Assistant surgeon in the Fifth Northumberland Fusiliers. I was mother, confessor and saviour to over a hundred men. Interesting occupation, war." His tone was bitter. "Hones one's surgical skills no end, what with hacking off limbs, sewing up empty eye sockets, pushing back spilled intestines. They have an amusing trick out there you know: they castrate a man and send him back to camp with his testicles sewn up in his mouth. They think it's funny. Fiends. I ended up killing the wicked devils myself. So much for the Hippocratic oath ... I believe I'll have another one, Tam. Landlord! A double. No, just bring the bottle."

"Well now, that be more like it," said the pirate. "That be ..."

"Pieces of eight!" shrieked Flint, dancing a jig on his shoulder. "Pieces of eight! Stand by to go about!"

All heads turned. The door was creaking slowly and noisily open. No one, since its creation, had ever seen fit to oil it. A dark head peeped through, disappeared again.

"Come in, my dear, we won't bite," said Silver silkily.

The girl emerged from behind the door.

"Bugger me backwards wi' a marlin spike," said the pirate under his breath, and then: "Come into the light where we can see 'ee."

She stepped forward hesitantly. The innkeeper glided along the wall behind her and closed the door without a sound. Tam, helping himself to more whisky, wondered, vaguely what had happened to the creak. Watson, who had risen to his feet as soon as she came in, pulled back a chair and begged her to sit down. She moved across the room with a swish of silken skirts, leaving a fragrance in her wake that set every man's pulse racing. She threw back long, raven locks and sat down, glancing around the room, nervous, but with a sharp challenge in her eyes. No one spoke. Sir Wilfred, who had also risen, took his seat again. It had been a long time since a woman had entered this room; seventy years at least. Silver struggled for the name. Lucia. That was it. Half-mad wench. Came from the Lammermuirs. Carried off long ago though. The memory was dim. The girl – she couldn't have been more than fifteen – was getting flustered.

"Isn't anyone going to speak? What is this place? Why am I here? Who are you all?" No one said a word. "I was washing the boys' clothes. It went … foggy. There was a castle and, oh God, thousands of horseless carriages. Only they didn't *look* like motor carriages, they looked more like … like slugs. The noise was unbearable."

"Pardon me, ma'am," said the old pirate, tearing his eyes from her bosom and flashing her a huge, ingratiating smile, which revealed a diminishing number of brown teeth and a single flash of gold. "This be the Salvation Inn. May I beg to interdooce my good friends here: Doctor John Watson, Master Tam o' Shanter and last, but in no wise to be thought least, Sir Wilfred of Ivanhoe." Each man stood up and inclined his head as he was named, but none spoke. Ivanhoe was white-faced and staring. Now that he saw her up close, the likeness was incredible! She was the image of …"

"My name is Wendy. How do you do? I'm the first Wendy that ever there was and you may call me 'Miss Darling'."

"An' I be Silver and you can call me Long John. Will ye do me the honour of joining me in a glass o' Spanish port? Pull up your chairs gents, this be a cause for celebration if ever there was such." Tam and John did so. Ivanhoe went back to his corner and sat down. He looked as though he didn't know where he was.

"Now then," said Wendy's self-appointed host, some time and several glasses of port later. "As to your question, which I freely admit I ain't answered yet, I was givin' you the wherewithal to put you at your ease afore I delivered the horrid truth. Which is to say I don't know where we be and I don't know exactly why we be 'ere, although I done a power o' guessin' over the years. Oh, I know we be in Edinburgh – that's where they all lived at one time or another – that's what 'olds it together. But that ain't *all* the truth of it, not by Flint's roastin' black soul it ain't. Howsobeit, I figure we be somewhere on the road atween Heaven and Hell and there be but one way out."

"And what, pray, might that be?" asked Wendy, who didn't know whether to be scornful or afraid. "And who are 'they'?"

"They be our father and our mother, Wendy. The authors of our being ye might say." He chuckled lewdly and eyed her cleavage.

"What do you mean?" said Wendy. "What on Earth do you mean?"

"Sin, my dear. Think on that. Mendin' our ways and movin' on."

"You're talking nonsense. Why are you talking nonsense? Why don't you answer my question?" She sounded tearful and slightly tipsy.

"By the powers, 'tis black as the Earl o' Hell's waistcoat out there an' wet as a seal's ... Landlord! Another glass for the young lady." The void that was the innkeeper wordlessly put another bottle on the table. They had all, long ago, ceased to pay him any attention, save to demand drink. Food was not part of the service: nobody had eaten a meal here for many years. Nobody had ever felt hungry.

"There's so much work to do," Wendy was saying. "Seven sets of clothes to wash and iron every week, twenty-one meals a day to prepare. We used to have servants for that and a nanny and everything. Just look at my hands. Peter's never there and I'm growing up and he isn't; Him and his stupid medicine. What's he afraid of? I've got ... needs now and he's just not ... well ... He's still got the body of a boy, you see. And the mind – fighting pirates for God's sake!" She was well away with the wine by now, a fact not un-remarked by John Silver. "Hook. He's obsessed with that damned old villain."

"Hook?" Silver spat on the floor. "Pah! Fop if ever I saw one, wi' 'is French wig an' 'is crew o' nancy boys. Two good legs an' 'e still couldn't whip a 'alf pint lad. One look at old Flint an' 'e'd 'a shited 'isself, an' Flint were afeared o' *me*! Beggin' your pardon ma'am for my colourful language." Wendy giggled and blushed and put a hand to her mouth.

"Ye're a liar an a thievin' rogue, Silver," piped Tam from across the table. The drink, as usual, was working its bad magic. "An ye stink nine man's eight forbye. Dae ye never think tae wipe the parrot shite aff yer shoother?" The old seaman laughed aloud.

"Buggered if you ain't right, Tam. I ain't 'ad a bath in three 'undred year. And what ails *ye*?"

"Me? Whit could ail me? Ah'm jist a comic." He shook his head as though in pain. His voice dropped to a whisper. "Sweet Christ! She was pumpin' blood frae her stump ... her een white an bulgin' frae her heid! I never saw sic fear in a beast. An yon fat bastard waitin at hame wi her rollin pin!" Tam's face crumpled and he fell forward onto the table, spilling his whisky. Within a minute, his sobs turned to snores.

Watson rose unsteadily and shuffled off in the direction of the privy. Silver poured Wendy another drink.

"The people around here must be terribly rich; they've all got motor carriages. And lots of the drivers were women. I'll bet they've all got nicer lives than I have. All I ever do is clean and cook and sew and make bloody breakfasts and bloody lunches and bloody suppers and wait in for Peter, please take your hand off my knee."

"Now m'dear, I knows what you needs an' I 'as it plentiful." The old pirate was intoxicated – by the smell of her, as well as by the liquor. *Fool, damn fool!* He thought, as he slid his hand up her thigh and lifted it to cup her breast. Wendy belted him across the face with the empty wine bottle and for the second time that day, he crashed to the floor. Cap'n Flint flew up into the high timbered ceiling and circled in the blackness, squawking and swearing horribly. Silver was beside himself with rage. Dripping blood and spitting oaths, he struggled back into his chair and reached for his crutch.

"You snotty bitch! I've split ice-arsed virgins like you from Providence to Valparaiso. Willin' or no an' by Hell I'll have you too!"

A bright, blinding blade hissed through the air in front of him and buried itself in the oak table with a crash that shook the inn to its rafters. The echo of it thundered around the inside of the pirate's skull till his head felt as though it would split.

"*Up, dog! Up, cur and defend thyself! Villain, black villain, to use a maiden so!*"

Ivanhoe's voice filled the universe. He was twelve feet tall and shining like gold. Silver was up like lightning, cutlass drawn and slashing at the air where the knight had stood a split second before. Long John Silver was many things, but he was not a coward. The knight had pulled the blade from the table and was circling the end of the other's cutlass with it, the table between them.

"Kill an old man wi' a timber leg would ye?" he bellowed at the knight. "Well then, come on! I ain't afeard o' ye or the Devil."

Ivanhoe froze. He glared at his foe in impotent fury. How he would love to carve this stinking pirate into small pieces. But John Silver, as always, had gone to the heart of the matter like a striking snake and fastened on the one thing that would save his life. The knight's code of honour would no more let him slaughter a one-legged man than let him murder the Holy Father of Rome.

"What the devil is happening here?" Doctor Watson had re-emerged and was struggling with the last button on his flies. "Good God, gentlemen, stop this, please. I beg of you." The last of the tension broke and both men slowly lowered their weapons. Wendy ran to the doctor and threw herself into his arms; a child running to daddy. She was half-drunk and confused and afraid.

"I want to go home," she wailed.

Watson patted her awkwardly on the back. "There there," he said. "There there."

Ivanhoe, the thankless hero, felt a stab of hurt. He sheathed his sword and went back to his corner, pausing for a moment to stroke her shining hair, as she sobbed against the doctor's chest.

"Rebecca," he murmured, and only Watson heard. Cap'n Flint settled back onto his master's shoulder. Tam was still asleep. The clock ticked. No one said anything for a long time. Silver knew he'd been lucky. The man had defeated seven Norman knights in one tournament: he'd have sliced him into sausage meat without breaking sweat, ageing though he was. And the sight and the sound of him! That was one of the strange things the Inn did from time to time. He took a long draught of rum. There was a time, long-ago, when he'd had two good legs and cork-heeled shoon and a mane of hair the colour of new gold, tied up with a bow of green velvet. By God she'd not have turned him down in those days. Damn Stevenson for a cold-hearted son of a whore!

"Need the bastard, though," he thought aloud. "Never get where I'm goin' without 'im, not the likes o' me. They'd never let me past the gate. Whatever it is I'm supposed to learn, don't 'ee think I've learned it by now? Don't ye think I've suffered? Be my soul still so black? *Come and get me, damn you!*" He was shouting at the ceiling and this finally woke Tam up.

"They aa pish in the same pot, John. Aa in it for the money." He shook his head sorrowfully. "Dae ye think auld Watty Scott gies a shite for yon puir auld bugger ower there in the corner? Or the likes ae me? 'You keep em poor and I'll keep em honest' he said yince tae yin o his aristocrat cronies when he wis shirra o Selkirk. But ye're richt; it's time we were awa. Time Rab came for *me* onywey." He sighed "He's probably oot drinkin. Or shaggin as wis aye his wont. Bastart!"

Watson had carried Wendy upstairs and was putting her to bed. Sir Wilfred couldn't for the life of him recall the inn ever having had an upstairs but he was nonetheless glad of it. The wench was the living image of Rebecca. He had chosen Rowena over her, but oh, the pain of parting! From one he loved, he now realised, just as well, though in different ways. The tears welled up in him but he fought them back down. His code forbade him utterly to weep.

"Know you, gentlemen," he said, "it is not an easy thing to be a knight. Most hate that which they perceive as perfect – it shines a harsh light upon their own shortcoming. Contrarily, they demand of me that very perfection they abhor. If once I fall short of it, they are on me like wolves. 'Tis a hard business when I cannot be a man but must needs be a saint. Reflect upon that when you bemoan your separate lots. There are times I would fain be such a villain as would see always to his own pleasure and be untroubled by any prick of conscience." He sighed. He was tired – tireder than he had thought possible. "'Tis pity, but thus am I writ and thus, alas, must I perforce endure."

"Pigshit!" said Long John Silver. He wrenched his chair around and spat in the fire. "You ain't no saint. Nor need you be no saint neither an' that's what *you* got to learn. Pompous bloody penguin! We *all* got to learn; that's why were here. That's why we keep comin' back night after night." The young wench upstairs would learn, he thought – quicker than any of them. She wouldn't be here long. Old Barrie'd be along to fetch her before a month had passed. She hadn't been chewed up enough by life to need much mending.

The fire had died to an ember. Tam was asleep again. The knight was staring into space, his mind turned inward once more.

"Hasn't heard a buggerin' word I said," muttered Silver. He hobbled to the window and looked out at the moving points of light and the odd buildings. A strange shore indeed he had fetched up on. But then again, what was really different? Not the greed, not the bustle and squalor, not the poverty, not the violence. People were shooting and bombing and disembowelling each other from Timor to Baghdad, from New York to Moscow, from Bogota to Peking, just as they'd always done. He crossed to the seaward window.

"Buggered that up good an' proper," he murmured to himself. "Fool, damn fool don't ye never learn?" He stood at the window for a long time, until the candles burned low, guttered and spat and went out. His pipe had long gone cold when the first grey glimmer of day appeared in the eastern sky.

A full sail, a rolling deck and a clean sea wind filling his lungs to bursting – how he longed for it! His soul was sick with waiting. Damn the man, why didn't he come?

Captain Flint croaked and nibbled his ear. He smiled affectionately and scratched the bird's head, cooing softly. Painfully, he reached for his hat, where it lay on the table and put it on. He still had on the coat that he seldom bothered, these days to take off. The innkeeper opened the great oak door as he reached it and closed it behind him as he stepped into the street.

The old pirate caused no comment as he lurched down the cobbled lane towards the docks. His three-cornered hat, long, wide-sleeved coat, his crutch and his parrot were as familiar to them as their own reflections. They were, after all, the ones who kept him alive. By their belief. He was part of their internal landscape. He was loved. He would be delivered. Someday, a pale, haggard man with a consumptive cough would touch him on the shoulder as he gazed, unknowing, out to sea. The man would beckon and Silver would follow. He would follow because the man knew the way. The way home.

Back at the inn, the fading figures rose, one by one, and left, drifting away into the grey morning until they were lost in the mist. The innkeeper closed the door, locked, bolted and barred it. One by one, he blew out the oil lamps and the remaining candles. He collected the glasses and the bottles and swept the debris of the night into the dead ashes of the fireplace. He went back to his accustomed place behind the bar and stood in the gloom for a long time. Then he took out a cloth and began, very slowly, to polish the scarred mahogany counter. His blind, flat face was utterly devoid of expression.

The Characters: *Long John Silver: the villain in Robert Louis Stevenson's* Treasure Island*; Tam o' Shanter: from Robert Burns's eponymous poem; Ivanhoe, hero of the Walter Scott's novel (Lucia, the 'Bride of Lammermuir' is also referred to in the story); Dr John Watson: friend and colleague of Sir Arthur Conan Doyle's detective, Sherlock Holmes; Wendy: friend of Peter Pan in J M Barrie's play of the same name.*

Note: the inclusion of apostrophes indicating missing letters in Long John Silver's dialogue (the mother tongue being English) and the omission of these from the words uttered by Tam (mither tongue being Scots) is deliberate!

John Holmes

Nein Nein Nein

I

My dad and me are just like chalk and cheese –
the antithesis of peas in a pod.
I'm easy-going but he's hard to please,
we share the same name but he calls me odd:

By, yer like 'em delinquent bloody poets,
don't say yer not ya cunt, cos ah can tell!

But his favourite line gets all my votes –

Yer a bloody fancy-nancy as well!
Readin' poetry's bloody unnatural
'n' lad, d'ye know what ah really think?
(This in my mind …)
Think? You can't think fuck all.

Ah think yer a bloody poof, ah swear pink!

Regular as clockwork he'd spout that line,
to me, his only son, aged nine, nine, nine.

II

But the years have passed and he's getting on –
ay, he's always had one hand on his HARP!
He's mellowed now for *Cunt* has become *John*
not *Poof,* not *Prick,* that tongue that once was sharp:

ah mind 'em days you used to pish the bed!

He never knew I did it out of fear.
But then, you did it too! I could've said –
the diff'rence was you did it through your beer.

We never spoke. I sulked within my tent.
(Even now he thinks that that means camping!)
But he's the one who'll soon be westward sent;
his pension book's near its final stamping –
and he knows too he's almost cooked his goose
while I care not, like Achi-bloody-lleus.

III

By, fucking comedian is it now?

Ah suppose yer think that's fucking funny?

Them Nein Nein Nein*'s 'bout me! ah don't know 'ow*
yer could write such stuff; from mi own son, eh!

Mind you, you don't really look much like me
'n' truth to tell ah've allus 'ad mi doubts;
'n' that poetry – it's not natural see
'n' 'ere's some more …

           (Dad's voice behind me shouts.)
Who do you think you are, Pam-fucking-Ayres?

(He always called me that time after time.)
But I no longer storm off up the stairs,
I get my own back on him with my rhyme:
and that is why I'm laughing like a drain
when he tries to read σὲ τὸν σοφιστήν

IV

Stanley, I have nothing to say! (Laurel and Hardy)

By, are you happy now? Ah bet you are!
Shoutin' at an old bloke, that's just yer style –
ah've allus known in life yer'd not get far
for ye've a bad streak as wide as a mile:

if only yer poor mum could see you now!

(Angels, dad said, took mum up to heaven.)

Ah'm sure she wouldn't want to see us row!

She left him when I was six, or seven.

Ay, his *angel* left – left us in the lurch,
me with him and him with his fags and drink.
Their unholy alliance, forged in Church;
this comedy of errors made me think –
you're like Laurel & Hardy 's what she'd say,
and she'd be right – I have nothing to say!

V

Ah'm not impressed wi all yer fancy words
'n' ah'll tell you what, all this rings a bell.
It's no wonder that you can't pull the birds
cos poet really means cunt 'n' ah can tell:

ah know cos once ah got poetry at school!

That surprised you, don't say you knew; as if!
Ah'm sure you think that ah'm a bloody fool,
well ah've read that poem by William Wordsmith –
that one 'bout a wandering golden cloud.

'N' that Tony Harris. He's another;
his poem v. should nivver 'ave been allowed:
with its fucking this and fucking other –

'n' there's you thinking ah know nowt, not me!
Thanks Dad for demonstrating – QED!

VI

QED? what the fuck is that to me
's what he said standing at the cooker,
he stirred his tin of beans (economy)
then turned and fell on me like a Stuka:

ah'm glad yer fucking mum now's dead and gone
'n' wi you a poet it's just as well!

(I knew his love for her was just a con
but to say that to me was a bombshell.)
I couldn't even look him in the eye,
the only sound the stirring of those beans,
I'd had enough and didn't want to try
to explain what a *fucking Poet* means.
This poem's for you Dad – all simple lines;
I won't make a meal of it – beans means Heinz!

VII

I was all at sea the day dad dropped dead
(his employ was both deck-had then navvy)
his last port of call was not in the Med
but was much closer to home, his lavvy:

ay, full-dead and with his pants at half-mast!

In truth, I near died myself with laughter
and how could I help it the way he passed
into the sunset, *the great hereafter.*
But I miss him for he was my father,
I miss him not in the way a son should,
not in a fond and loving way, rather;
to write him wrong as I choose, can and could.
So goodbye dad, here ends my *rapportage* –
I'm waving you off, *bon*-fucking-*voyage*!

Johnnie Walker

Danny Gillan

I make a point of never drinking before 8 o'clock. To be fair, I'm rarely up that early, so it's usually closer to ten before I crack open my first can of lager.

When I was a bairn my dad used to tell me that an hour's sleep before midnight was worth two after. I reckon that was a load of crap, but I have found that an hour's drinking before midday adds a far more acceptably surreal quality to the day than two hours in the afternoon.

I enjoy being drunk in the morning. The earlier the better, I say. Whether I'm just up or haven't been to my bed yet, there's something strangely satisfying about wandering the streets in an alcoholic haze while other people go about their business.

There's the paper boy, saggy-eyed and miserable as he delivers his daily dose of bad-tidings; there's me, happily oblivious to the world's 'issues'. There's the deliveryman in his delivery-van with the rolls for the bakery; there's me, sitting comfortably in a doorway, glad that I never seem to get hungry any more.

I like my life. It's very simple, very easy. I'm not stupid, I know I probably won't last as long as most. I'm okay with that. The kids call me 'Johnnie Walker'. Sometimes I'm flattered, sometimes I'm not. I struggle to remember my real name half the time, so Johnnie Walker does the job well enough.

They mean well. A couple of them invite me into their pubs before opening time and give me a bite to eat and a cup of tea now and then. I'm not allowed in when they're open, though. I understand that. They're good kids. It's funny; these days, my best friends and my biggest persecutors are kids.

I'm fifty-two, or thereabouts, and my life is all about kids. Again.

Constance. It was a beautiful name for a beautiful child. Diane never looked lovelier than she did that day in the hospital. She was shouting and crying, she was sweating and swearing, she was cursing and counting, counting down the seconds till our angel appeared.

This angel. My constant Constance. That's what keeps me happy; the memory of constant little Constance. She was only three when they came and took her away. They were right to do it. I was a mess back then, so was Diane. Constance was a wee baby, she shouldn't have had to see that.

Dirty needles, that's what got Diane in the end. I think I remember the actual needle that killed her. We were at a party in the Gorbals. We hadn't been out for ages, but we were celebrating.

"This'll do," she said, picking a syringe from the pile in the kitchen. Usually we were careful, but Diane was pissed. "You want?" I shook my head. Most times I would have jumped right in there, but some guy had just given me a jazzer of a smoke in the living room, so I wasn't ready for another hit just yet.

We went through to the bedroom for a bit of peace. Nobody seemed to use the bedrooms at those parties. I remember watching jealously as Diane cooked the score. Her arms were still as a ghost as she held the lighter under the soup spoon. I heard the sizzle as the ten quid deal we'd bought dissolved. It has a strange smell, burning heroin. Sort of like death, but easier.

She sucked it up and plunged it in. I'm fairly sure Diane killed herself that night, but her grimace-like grin as she sank slowly backwards onto the bed showed she at least thought she had enjoyed it.

Nine months later, when she actually died, she didn't look quite so happy. Losing your options, your child and your immune system tended to do that.

I gave up the drugs after Diane died. Twenty years straight without a fix, and proud of it. It's just the drinking for me now. You know where you are with the drinking. It's easy enough to tell when you've had enough and need a bit of sleep. With drugs, you never knew what state you were going to end up in, especially with the crud those wankers used to cut it with. Sometimes you could smell the soap powder before you even opened the wrap.

"Morning, Johnnie."

"Hi, son." It's one of the kids from Molly Malone's. I think his name's Tommy. He's told me his name before, but my memory doesn't always work too well these days.

"You need a cuppa?" He's one of the good kids, Tommy. Not like those other wee bastards.

"Well, my boy. I've never been the sort of man who refuses an honestly extended invitation, as you well know." I like to put on a bit of a show for the good kids, give them a bit of a flourish? I'm a born entertainer, really.

"In you come then, mate."

I wait patiently for young Tommy to unlock the doors and switch the lights on. I take up my usual seat at the back, away from the windows, while Tommy goes behind the bar and switches on the coffee machine. It's got a tap that gives out hot water for tea, apparently.

"It'll take five minutes to heat up. D'you want a look at the paper?" Tommy offers me the folded up *Daily Record* he's had under his arm.

"You are both a scholar and a gentleman."

Tommy laughs. "No worries, Johnnie. I need to nip downstairs for a minute, I'll sort out your tea when I get back. You OK on your own?"

"A thinker such as myself is never truly alone, young Thomas."

Tommy laughs again, disappearing through the door marked 'Private'.

When you dress for the outdoor life like I do, it can get a bit hot on the rare occasions you find yourself inside. Still, the cloak on your back is your truest friend and shouldn't be lightly discarded, even briefly.

I unfold young Tommy's paper on the table, quickly digesting the only information of interest to me. One of the joys of my lifestyle is that my daily concerns rarely relate to those of the wider, newspaper-buying population. I do occasionally like to be reminded of what day it is. Just occasionally, mind.

Today is Thursday, the ninth of November.

There's no sign of Tommy's return, and I get up and take a wander. The coffee machine is starting to rumble reassuringly, and I'm looking forward to my cup of tea. Tommy has been known to throw in a roll and sausage when the mood takes him, too. Not that I need or expect it, but it shows the boy has a good heart. Plus, I do know I should eat a bit of something now and then. It's only sense, isn't it?

I go up to the burbling silver machine for a closer look. It's all dials and knobs and tubes, beyond me. In my day it was a kettle with a whistle and a gas hob, if you were lucky.

While I'm reading the metal plaque on the top of the machine that says 'Pompeii' in fancy gold writing, I give the door of the cupboard it's sitting on top of a wee nudge with my knee. The door swings open a couple of inches. I've noticed that about young Tommy – he's always forgetting to lock things. He'll get himself in trouble one of these days if he's not careful.

I crouch down for a look. There are two bottles of Johnnie Walker Red Label, but I ignore them. There's vodka and gin, but I'd rather not, given the choice. At the back I spot a bottle of Courvoisier brandy.

When Tommy comes back I'm at my table again, looking at the paper. I can feel the heft of the brandy swaying against my shin from the inside lining of my coat. The cloak on your back.

"D'you fancy roll and sausage, Johnnie?"

"Ah, your good manners are matched only by your generosity, my young friend. It would be churlish of me to refuse."

Tommy soon joins me at my table, bearing gifts of steaming tea and savoury smelling, bread-wrapped square-sliced.

"It's getting chilly out there, Johnnie. Will you be OK for the winter?"

I'm touched by his concern. "I'll be fine, young man. I'm an old hand."

"I know, but you're not getting any younger."

I decide to embark on an experiment. "And how young would you surmise I in fact am, Thomas?"

Tommy sighs. "Christ, I don't know, Johnnie. Sixty? Sixty-five?"

The results of the experiment are disappointing, but the boy can't be blamed for that. "Perhaps the truth of the matter might surprise you," I say.

As I say goodbye to Tommy, thanking him for his kindness (and mentally for his unwitting generosity), I ponder on the date. The ninth of November.

I tried not to let it show in front of young Thomas, but this date means something. It's one of the few dates I choose to remember. I know how difficult the rest of this day is going to be and am glad of the comforting weight pulling at me from the bottom of my coat.

On this day every year, I think about Diane and Constance. On this day every year I find myself less able than usual to interact with others. I find myself less able to beg, to please, to entertain.

Fortuitously, Tommy came along early enough this morning for me to still be sociable, to be entertaining, and allowed me to purloin a source of support for the true horror of the day that I know is still to come.

I make my way down the lane behind the Theatre Royal. Everyone deserves to have a home – and this is mine. I pull the rags, the papers and the black plastic bags of rubbish off my mattress. I'm normally careful about this process, aware that I will need this camouflage again before too long, but today I don't care. I may lose some of it when the council men come along to empty the bins, but there's always more garbage to be found. Always.

I like people, I'm a people person. I like to talk, I like to joke, I like to put on a show for my customers. Today I'm having a day off, though. The ninth of November is my one day off, has been for twenty years.

I get myself settled. The smells and the rats and the shit stopped getting to me a very long time ago. After taking out my bottle of brandy, I wrap all three of my overcoats around me. I pull my woollen gloves out of my pocket and put them on. This year is better than most. I've had a cup of tea and a bite to eat. The sky is dry. I've got a decent bottle. It's cold, but not as cold as some years. My new mattress is much comfier than the last one was, too. I'm all set.

I'm all set to drink myself to sleep, hopefully before it gets too bad. I open the bottle. Courvoisier, this is a very good year. The aroma of the brandy supersedes the stink of my home, and I bring the bottle to my nostrils, savouring its sweet sharpness for a few seconds.

The ninth of November.

I take the first swallow. It's glorious. I can't remember the last time anything burned my throat, but this does. It's a good burn, a happy burn. I close my eyes as that first mouthful completes its journey from my throat to my belly. The heat, Jesus, the heat. It's as close to heaven as I'll ever see, but it feels like hell. If hell burns, I want to go there.

The ninth of November, the day constant little Constance was born, all those years ago. My Constance, my Diane. My life, my love. My past, my past.

The ninth of November, the day Diane and I went to a party to celebrate Constance's third birthday. The day Diane picked up a needle and said "this'll do". I can't even remember who was looking after the baby for us that night.

The ninth of November. Remember, remember.

"Dad?"

I open my eyes. I must have fallen asleep. The light has changed and the brandy is half-finished on my lap, held by my listless left hand.

There's a woman standing over me, in front of me. She has blonde hair, and the face of an angel. "Dad?"

Oh God, stop torturing me.

"Dad? It's me, it's Constance," she says.

How can this be possible? How can she have found me, a tramp, a vagrant, a person of no current abode?

"I found you, dad," she says. "I found you again." I see she is crying, perhaps with joy, perhaps not.

I finally feel able to speak. "Constance? Connie? You're here? You found me?"

Constance nods. "I found you, Dad."

"Why?"

"Because you're my dad, and I love you."

"Jesus, girl. You don't even know me. Look at me." I try not to let her see my tears. I pretend she's just another customer, like young Tommy.

"I don't care. Do you know how many years I've spent looking for you? You're my father. I want you to come home with me. Let me look after you." The child seems distraught. A girl as beautiful as she is doesn't deserve tears.

I catch her eyes with mine and make her face still. That's one of the powers parents have and never lose. I hold her gaze until she crumbles.

"Not again, Dad. Don't do this again."

"You need to go, Constance. You need to go home. Forget about me. Please forget. You were supposed to forget."

"But Dad!" Constance is crying. I hate to see that.

"Constance, go. Go. For Christ's sake, just go."

"At least let me get you some food."

"I've eaten my fill for today, Constance."

"How about just talking to me, then?"

"It would be best if you went home now, Constance." I lower my head as I say this, unable to meet her terrifying, miserable, gorgeous eyes.

"But ..."

"Just go, Constance. Please, just go home."

I watch as Constance reluctantly turns and leaves the lane, my lane.

Why can't she forget?

I make sure I'm in a different lane every year, but she still finds me. Every year since she turned twenty she's done this; every year on her birthday she tracks me down and reminds me that I had another life, a life I failed at.

I failed Diane, I failed Connie. At least now I don't hurt so much.

Why does she have to keep reminding me? My constant little Constance.

I need a drink. At least there's some brandy left.

Danny Gillan's first novel *Will You Love Me Tomorrow* was Scottish Region winner in the Undiscovered Authors 2007 competition run by Discovered Authors and published by them October 08. The novel went on to win third place in the UK-wide competition.

James Spence

Much of my subject matter in art can be traced to childhood. In 1938, I was taken by my uncle to an open-air boxing match in Glasgow. It was evening and the white bodies of the fighters were silhouetted in brilliant light. I recall my horror at seeing a mass of crimson blood covering the face of one who continued to battle as if nothing had happened. In 1988, as a delayed catharsis, I produced a series of large woodcuts of boxers, at various stages of *in extremis*.

In 1939, I was evacuated to Tullynestle, Aberdeenshire. My sister and I left from Bridgeton Cross station, some children seen off by mothers wearing slippers and hair curlers – worn almost always by many working class women in those days, as if constantly anticipating a special occasion.

Arriving at Alford, the evacuees were placed in a church hall, and the local people chose the children to be billeted with them. The minister's wife selected my sister and me and we stayed at the manse; but after she discovered she could get twice the allowance by privately taking some English evacuees, we were downgraded to stay with the gravedigger – a large kindly man with heavy studded boots curving forwards and upwards. When electing a new minister he voted for the biggest preacher, as by tradition he inherited his worn suits.

Aged 14, I contracted TB and spent 4 years in hospital at Inverurie. Most of my fellow patients were military men who taught me much more than school had to offer. Some had been POWs in Germany, one had fought Franco in the Spanish Civil War. I learned chess, studied Spanish, and took a correspondence course on art. I found that my interest in art increased daily – especially given the endless supply of willing models. At 17 I was sent to a Glasgow hospital for a major operation on the diseased lung. From there I contacted Jefferson Barnes (registrar of Glasgow School of Art) who advised me on preparing a portfolio. I decided to make art a career but needed Highers for entry. After my operation I took a correspondence course for the London Matric and applied to GSA. Barnes interviewed me for entry and recommended me on the strength of my watercolour portraits (of fellow patients).

Art School was an anti-climax, with little intellectual life, but Alasdair Gray and I founded a debating society which won second prize in the Observer Trophy – and we got Hugh MacDiarmid to speak to us. But we seemed to spend the first two years endlessly drawing boxes and making pointless colour charts.

In third year, meeting teachers like Donaldson, Squires, Mary Armour and Benno Schotz, the doors of the imagination finally opened. I spent summer 1956 at Hospitalfield Art College Arbroath, tutored by Mclaughlin Milne whose knowledge of early Scottish artists included Peploe and Cadell. He had travelled widely and in the South of France knew Fergusson and Sigonsac.

In 1957, unhappy with the art scene in Glasgow, James Morrison, Anda Paterson (who became my wife) and I founded the Young Glasgow Group.

consisting of 13 like-minded young artists, mainly friends and colleagues from GSA. Eager to paint Scottish landscape, I decided to buy a van. A dealer at Bridgeton Cross, a heavily-built Irishman with a charming avuncular manner, offered me a Bradford. When he showed me the engine the bonnet fell on the floor, but I was assured that a few rivets would put this right. I pointed to a 3-inch gap on the rear doors. Hand on my shoulder, he said, "There's nothing worse than lack of ventilation when sleeping in a van." I added that I'd yet to pass my driving test, his response was to prod, with his boot, a recumbent figure sleeping amongst old tyres in a dimly-lit corner of the room. "My mechanic here is a very patient man. Not only will he teach you to drive, but he will ensure that you have a mechanically perfect vehicle."

Later, with Glasgow Group members Ian McCulloch and Ewen McAslan, I journeyed to Morar in the "mechanically perfect vehicle". The brakes were non-existent and I floated into a Morris Minor in Fort William. After that I tried to adjust the brakes. On the precipitous one-track road above Loch Sheil, descending rapidly towards a hairpin bend, we met a Mallaig fish lorry: The brakes had not improved. Loch Sheil to my left, granite cliff to my right, I aimed for the cliff, hit a boulder and by a miracle squeezed past the lorry. The van rear doors flew open and the road became strewn with our provisions. The van was still hurtling towards the bend; Ewen made the sign of the cross and quietly prayed; Ian resigned himself to fate with stoic fortitude. We negotiated the bend and the van stopped on an incline. After final adjustments of the brakes we continued on to Morar Sands to make camp. The evening light over the islands was a magical drama of an unreal world. The heavens burned with myriad colours and the islands shimmered in translucent turquoise. All previous experience of skies was as nothing compared to this visual paradise.

In 1959 I visited Spain for the first time. Having read Rose Macaulay's *Fabled Shore*, we stayed in Denia. We visited Madrid where I saw my first bull fight. Both man and beast are tested in this primordial contest. The first impression is one of carnival. The sand is a brilliant pink, the colourful *cuadrilla* pageant of *picadors*, *banderilleros*, and *toreros* enter to the sound of *paso dobles*. When you see a bull lift a picador and his horse off the ground you realise his incredible power. The impression of carnival changes to one of increasing horror as the magnificent animal is tormented and tortured, ending in humiliation and painful death. The bull is rarely killed cleanly, taking many sword thrusts, and often only dispatched by severing the spinal cord with the dagger.

For 30 years I have made studies of the bullfight in watercolour, oil, etching, and mezzotint. Despite my fascination with the subject, I have never been able to reconcile myself to the manner of the killing.

Now, Anda and I spend winters in Spain or Portugal, both countries are rich sources of material for the artist. Anda studies the 'Eternal Peasant' and I find endless stimulation sketching the landscape and mountain villages.

James Spence

Ben Lomond – Watercolour

Winter Solstice

Stac Polly – Oil

Nerja – Watercolour

Bull of the Sierras

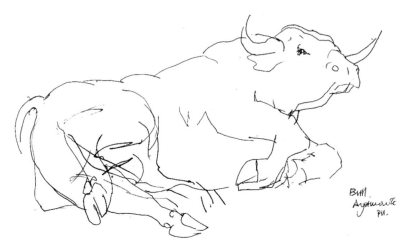

Bull Ayamonte – Pen Drawing

Arab Waterwheel, Cordoba – Oil

Almond Trees, Arcos de la Frontera – Oil

Man and Horse

Old Wrestler

Champion – Woodcut

Fallen Picador

Down and Out – Woodcut

Trawlers, Pittenweem

Roseneath and Argyll Mountains – Oil

Gerda Stevenson

Autumn Night

Leaves wheel at me out of the black
and skitter across pale sheets
that sigh on the line like tired lungs;
the pup tosses a stray quince
in the cold dew, while sweet steam rises
from the ones that reached the pot,
my mother a stooped blur
behind her kitchen window
as she stirs another year's harvest.

The Catwalk

"Take care round this bend,"
warned my father, always,
at sight of the tallest pine.
"Single file!"
And the dolls' china tea-set
chinked in its basket,
as our toes detected
culprit roots
on the Catwalk path
above the gorge.
"Remember *those* sisters."

I'd picture their eyes,
like the startled stars
of forget-me-nots
that grow on the bank
above the spot
where they tripped –
their dresses as blue –
and plunged
hand in hand
in the heedless '20s
through careless arms
of hazel and birch,
feet fluttering
a desperate Charleston
they'd never dance.

Child in the Woods

You dip from sight
behind dark pines
on a steep bend
in the glen's well.

I wait, as always,
while you catch up,
listen for your answer
to my call,
for a stick's crack,
a stone's fall;
I'm a deer or dog
all ears for you.

Then, at last, the signal sounds:
your new yellow mouth organ
threads the air in plaintive strains,
your white face rises over the ridge,
small moon cradled in low-slung boughs,
and my love rises at the gift of you.

Two Horses Against a Hill

Two horses against a hill,
shoulder to shoulder,
one faces East, the other West,
and I think of us –
how we can be,
sometimes, at our best:
opposites, yet close enough
to cradle each other's different worlds
in a wide arc of peripheral vision.

Linton Power Cut

The wires were aa doon wi the blizzard's virr,
black wicks stitterin intae life ahint
ilka door an frostit winnock, the lenth
o the snaw-happed street. The wind drapped and sooched
a dwaiblie braith, taigelt o the day's fecht;

the Gifford clock's greetin face wis steekit
at twenty past seeven, when the news swyped
the stern-lichtit lift: "A lorry's skytit
and tummelt its load – oranges bleezin
doon the brae, gowd frae Seville in the snaw!"

Santa Maria la Real

Siesta in Pamplona, and snow falls slow
as the cathedral gates begin to close.
Three blue pines, caged in the cloister's
lancet arches, reach for their square
of laden sky, and receive flake upon flake
with the same mute grace that Santa Maria
la Real accepts the chill of her silver robes
applied by the smith to her wooden flesh –
the carved Virgin of Navarre.

Silent, she rests at the city's heart,
a distant star in a cobalt dome,
remote from all show of devotion,
flanked by the royal tomb's
padlocked spikes – so high
on her throne we can only believe
in the subtle line of her painted cheek,
in the nestling infant on her knee.

A door booms through shadowed stone;
votive flames shudder in their corner shrine,
and lingering pilgrims steal a last glance
at the lone priestess, the miniature queen,
whose eyes catch mine from the postcard rack
on the way out. I make my purchase,
and study her features, as I step
into the snow-hushed street:
a peasant girl's quiet face,
under the load of a mighty crown;
no fear for the future marks her brow;
no trace in her gaze of the sad tale to come –
just the gentle certainty of breast milk.

Ar-ta and Peem
Kenneth Stephen

"*Eightyshillintom!*"

Tom pulled out a clean glass, slippery from the brush-wash, and glanced at Arthur. Arthur was soft in the head, half here, half somewhere only Arthur could be, but he knew what lipstick tasted like. To everyone, Arthur was Arthur. To Arthur, Arthur was Ar-ta. He had brought the cold in. Tom saw it in his bloated pink face as he held the tumbler to light for smears. The air carried with it a smell of the coast as the door closed.

"Cold the night, eh, Arthur?"

Arthur stared somewhere between the pocked carpet and the neon bar sign, struggling to get a thigh-hold on a burst stool.

"You and Peem out for the duration?"

"*Dunno!*"

Tom watched as Arthur turned the fleshy part of his palm in the round of his eye.

"*Somethinswrong!*" Tom didn't care much for an audit of Arthur's woes. He couldn't possibly decode Arthur's mind. Plus, if Arthur sat down, he could watch MTV again. "*Peem'snoright! Been wheekinlots!*"

Arthur interrupted his own flow; delivered a terse clap to the Boxer's snout.

"*Christ sidoonpeem!*" Peem whinnied. "*Sitsillydug!*"

The chain of Peem's lead clanked the brass footrest. He struggled no more. Behind, the Killers and a pogo of bodies were going Kasbah on the plasma. From Vegas to Scotland's East Coast, the sound muted for the greyhounds. Dougal Mearns crumpled his betting slip beneath the phone cubicle – another Friday-sized dent in the wage packet. His flies hung open. Half in shadow, Ali Meechen examined a pork chop, brought from a Somerfield bag and laid out on the varnished table. Arthur jiggled his girth onto the stool and balanced. With a salmon-coloured finger, he chased drips down the Bud Ice font. Tom watched as a fold of his belly flab found a groove on the walnut bar-edge. The eighty pump wheezed bronchial froth. Arthur was making himself comfortable. For a rural town boozer, with a piddle of regulars and a small window of pre-disco sales, Arthur's trade was vital. The only problem was the thing Tom couldn't handle: Arthur had that look that slow folk had.

It was as if Arthur was forever waiting for something, some interaction that could never happen because the stare itself forbade it. It left Tom cold. He wished there were glasses to collect. Before the smoking ban, at least he could have wiped ashtrays with a chamois. He never expected customers would fail to grasp the basic dynamic. Tom did not – and never would – serve Arthur beer because he liked him. Arthur wants beer. Arthur pays. Arthur gets beer. Tom is the conduit. It was business. It did not entitle Arthur to follow him in the street or stand really close to him. Business – always just business, wherever they were – even if all his Edinburgh Management degree had got him was a franchise boozer in the back hells of Angus. He was not bitter. Cried a few times after lock-up but nothing he couldn't handle. And maybe, one day, something might happen, something to make him feel alive again, like he used to feel not all that long ago. In the days before he knew people like Arthur.

He shook some peanuts into a bowl and slid them along the bar. He was sure Arthur saw it coming, but the bowl hit off his elbow.

"On the house, Arthur. Think there's some air in the pipes. Eighty'll be a minute."

"*'Sa'right! TakyirtimeTom!*"

Arthur shifted his stare towards three girls who had strutted in. They were underdressed for the icy blast, the first of the pre-clubbers. Tom relaxed. An excuse to remove himself from Arthur's attention. He resented the way Arthur made him feel trapped. He would never forget the afternoon Arthur drooled a line of saliva onto the bar. It glistened in the sun-shaft through a window, suspended from a white crumb of mucus in the crease of his mouth. Arthur just stared. Stared and smiled widely at Tom. And Tom could not escape the presence of the spit wherever his eyes went. The line remained unbroken until Arthur moved and it snagged and fell away on his jacket. Arthur sat by the bandit, completely unaware, a melting icicle clinging to the end of his chin. During Tom's break, the image kept returning, in the faces in the paper. Princess Stephanie of Monaco. Craig Brewster. He left his tuna baguette half-wrapped in cling film, a few bites out of it. It wasn't the thought of the spit that made him sick. It was the impenetrable void in Arthur's eyes. To have only one shot at life but barely know you were alive enough to live it.

Tom dabbed eighty slop off the glass. Rips of beer-mat were scattered like confetti, exactly where he was stretching over to rest the pint. Arthur had been tearing it. The glass wouldn't sit right on the sodden circle with the corners bent up. Some of the beer slabbered, as the glass rested at an angle. It was uneven. It irritated Tom. He picked at the shreds of beer-mat. Inside, Arthur's presence was grating on him. Arthur, unaware, stared moronically at the ladies. They were debating vantage points, their accents thicker than the darkness outside. Sometimes carloads from Dundee would come for a sniff. The local women circled them like ravenous gulls around chips. The seabirds up the coast used to follow boats. The only fish these days fell from a bag, with batter and sauce. "Is that everything, Arthur?"

Arthur didn't move. Just scratched at a red rash on his arm. Harder and harder. Pricks of rosy blood spotted the skin.

"Arthur?"

"GrispsfirPeem! Anajaramussels. FirAr-ta!"

Arthur's choice intrigued Tom. Normally Peem took scampi fries. Then again, Peem wasn't right today. Tom heard the dog pine. No one really knew how Arthur got Peem. Peem just turned up. The catering rep said he saw Arthur sitting with Peem on the bench by the Church every morning, yattering away to him. They'd still be there when he drove past at lunch-time.

"Just a poor saft bugger," he said, holding out the board for Tom to sign. The Christies were the oldest farmers in the area. "The only een that cared for that boy was the mither. She's been deid six years. Sad. Bloody sad, ye ken."

Tom watched him shaking his head as he secured the van doors. Sometimes, when alone, Tom remembered the resignation in the rep's voice.

Momentarily, the smell of perfume had transported Tom back to the buzz of the city. But Arthur's jerking movements, behind him in the mirror, broke the dream. Through the lime letters of Amigo's Bar, Arthur was battling the crisps. Limp forefingers negated thumbs. Tom turned to watch.

"You winning, Arthur?"

Arthur didn't speak. The concentration made his breath vibrate in his nose. He raged at his impotence. *"Firfuksake!"*

Tom cut the small-talk. He repeated his line, 'You winning, Arthur?' in his own head. Was it really insensitive? He turned it over and over. Everything was relative. In Arthur's life, this was hard. Crisps were hurdles, sealed in bags to be beaten. He took a nip glass and pressed it under the vodka optic, did his best to silence the click at the end of the shot. On the screens Beyonce swivelled her hips, all rhythm and synchronicity, but Tom watched Arthur. Arthur was a science in himself. The colours of the bandit flickered in the mussel jar. Arthur lodged his plump tongue between his teeth, positioning his fingers for the final try. Ripping open, the crisps spilled erratically over the bar onto the floor for Peem, followed by the bag. Arthur breathed out, hard. Tom heard a sniffing of the foil but there was no usual lapping of tongue by Arthur's trainers. Arthur looked down at his feet and Tom watched him move his arm back and forth. He must have be stroking Peem, he thought.

"Whatswrong? WhatsimatterPeem?"

It was the first time Tom had heard emotion in Arthur's voice.

Tom pressed the sound up a notch on the remote and turned to slug his vodka. He was drowning out guilt. Maybe he shouldn't just brush Arthur aside. Maybe Arthur was genuinely hurting about Peem. The way other folk hurt. One girl stood up, a slick black anaconda with a tummy ring. Tom let the thought go. It was only Arthur. There was something more pressing in his midst. The girls were talking gin and tonics. One rocked a black high-heel along painted toenails. She was under age but there was something thoroughly dirty about her that he liked. His brain had already computed he would not throw her out. The thought of the power he had set his heart cycle faster.

"Howmuchtom?"

Tom turned to see Arthur's insane smile hold him frozen. The possibility of the moment seemed to shrink. With cupped hand, Arthur was shovelling mussels. Tom watched discoloured fragments of fish-flesh sucked in. It was the slow look that turned his stomach. Arthur rubbed the vinegar on his thighs. With a quick dunk in the sink and a squeeze, Tom skimmed the bar-top with a cloth. Any minute the girl would order. The last thing he wanted was for the place to stink and daft Arthur sitting farting in the middle of it. As the soft buttons of the till gave in to his fingertips, Tom felt anticipation building inside him. Surely, after three years, something was going to happen?

"Arthur. Four pound five."

Arthur's first pound coin spun golden on the bar. Everything else had the shock of inevitability. The girl's shoe touched the first step. Tom told him.

"I'll get it later, Arthur." He said it again. But something was moving Arthur.

"Fuckinbreeks!" he shouted.

The girl walked down another step.

"Arthur man, it's OK."

Arthur plunged his hand, deeper. The pocket was too tight. Tom saw a red crease deepen on Arthur's hand, his face blotchy with exertion.

"Arthur, Christ's sake leave it, man," he pleaded. "You'll give yourself a heart attack."

Below all that thickness in Arthur, something was pushing him on.

"It'scomingnoo."

The thing pushing him was Tom. Good Tom. Ar-ta won't let Tom down.

Tom reached out but Arthur's wrist had gone. From being suspended on the stool, Arthur was on the carpet beside Peem. From somewhere, there came a scream. The girl froze and dropped her purse. Vinegar trickled down her shins. Arthur lay still. Around him, the splintered legs of the stool. Sharp pear halves of glass lay by his face. Peem gave a high pitched whine. He licked at the flow of red blood on Arthur's cheek. Chewed a mussel then discarded the glob, moaning in pain beside him. Slowly Arthur opened his eyes. Tom stared into the giant dopey orbs and he saw it for himself. Where the milky void was, there was also humiliation. The stare had dual settings. Switched to nothing or shame and Arthur bore the shame alone. If he could have, Tom would have held him like a mother. He didn't.

"Am sorry, Tom."

"It's alright, Arthur."

Arthur motioned to the broken chair. "Am so sorry." He released his fingers. Three pound coins fell out.

Rob MacKenzie

Psalm

Lord, when will you dull the splendour of light
that hides you?

If I were to strip the earth of cover,
snap the mirrored glasses,
cut the curtains into ribbons,
would I not find the face of another earth
and then another, each more microscopic
and brutal than the last?

call to the sky and the sky
will melt the tree tops
like a shadow

If I were to trim back the beech tree
that overhangs the hedge,
with each slice, a world would fall in
on itself – ants, spiders,
a sandstorm of microscopic eggs blown into
a cardboard box. Where is
redemption, Lord? Who could be saved
if you did not hear their cries?

call to the dust and the dust
will cloud over your vision
like a breath

If I were to chop it down, and the sun
rained on the dry grass without check,
and the stump bore brutal witness

to its absence, and in the gap it left,
nothing new would grow,
would you break your silence?

call to the silence and the echo
will speak in your voice
like a minor god

If I were to surrender my axe
and keep vigil by the trunk,
and become like the earth, microscopic
and brutal, containing others
and contained by others, would you

speak a word, would you speak
a word, would you, would
you speak a word, would you speak a

tremble, earth, at the Lord's coming,
as shadows become pools of water,
and solid forms, flowing springs

Scotlands

Just when we think we have arrived, the coach jolts forward
from the Sorley MacLean Appreciation Society Picnic,

which once had been the terminus on this excursion
through healthy weeds, peat bogs, and everlasting rain.

Although we still hear mouth music in the distance,
the accent is American, the language a kind of English,

and the entire population is queuing round the clock
for pizza, chicken vindaloo, and deep-fried Mars Bar.

At six degrees, it's the warmest day in Falkirk this year,
but the coach shoots past for the Museum of Scotland

and a quick dose of reality – our miserable record of defeats
in battle against ourselves. When we emerge,

Edinburgh has disappeared, and a choir of Tartan Tories
improvise God Save The Queen on Culloden Field,

while we photograph the grass. "Much too green,"
someone says, which induces a predictable backlash

from the ecumenical contingent. Everyone now feels
discriminated against and half the passengers board

a ferry to Nova Scotia. We hear many have drowned
by the time we reach Glasgow's suburban sprawl

and there is bitterness, bitterness against those who left,
bitterness at the speedbumps, bitterness that the Scots

Dictionary compiler has bonded with the monoglot
tour guide, bitterness at being left behind, perhaps to die

in these plush leather seats, bitterness at the angle
we approach the Sacred Cows statuette, but nevertheless

enchantment at the world beyond the windows – on one side
a row of builders' bums and flash women, and on the other

a child crouched by the bonnie bonnie banks of Loch Lomond,
blowing dandelion clocks, which fan out on a tail wind's

whistle-stop tour of common ground, each fibre waiting for
the sudden drop, for a patch of earth in which to root itself.

The Iona Nunnery

George MacLeod and his team of men –
joiners, ministers, miners and brickies –
restored Columba's abbey stone by stone:
an active worship space and pilgrim station,
and a monument to monks who wrote down
accounts of discipline, ethics, miracles.

Nearby the nunnery remains a ruin.

Each Wednesday prayers are offered
for women whose names go unrecorded,
whose houses are never rebuilt,
for feminism, for visibility.

The nuns do not care.

They lived only to serve their God
behind walls, anonymous, in silent cells.
The wind breathes among the stones,
each a lost, unlamenting voice.

Let the nuns walk their long aisles.
Let their mouths close behind their veils.
Let what remains of their house fall to rubble.

Crossing the Border

There's a sign at the side of the road welcoming us
to Northumberland District, but no suggestion
that we have moved from one existence
into another.

On our return, the border is announced
one mile back in preparation for three Saltires
marking the event, each raised on poles
at different heights. That's just the official ceremony.

A Saltire flies from a burnt-out caravan fifty yards on,
from a hotel roof, from a petrol station draped in tartan,
from fences, gateposts, conservatories.

By some oversight, the sheep have not been painted
blue and white, and no one has installed a video loop
in life-size widescreen as permanent homage
to Archie Gemmill's goal against Holland in 1978,
but there's no doubting where we are.

Further on, nothing appears to have changed.
The hills are green, cows munch in the rolling fields,
clouds shadow us up the motorway.

But there is an inner sense of arrival, of being home.
Going the other way, there's no sense
of ever having left.

Safari

Safari was a lifetime ambition, she said,
although she'd never mentioned it
in five years of marriage.

In early days when love covered up our lack
of frankness, I might have mentioned how
she hates humidity, meaning
I hate humidity, but these days
we nod assent to most things.

So today we gawp at an elephant herd
through binoculars
we snatch in turn. "Look at the babies,"
I say, and she looks at the haze
while I look at the babies.

Our guide explains the thinness of skin,
how elephants cool the day in mud,
how a young one sticks to its mother's shadow
to avoid sunburn.

I pass the binoculars. The world
resets at a safe distance; the space between us
and them makes it likely
we will muddle through
without incident.

"They're beautiful," I say, meaning
she is beautiful. She doesn't turn.
Her eyes focus on thinness, mine
on distance. We both see
the same elephants.

The Silent Authors
Fritha Waters

The Wall was the only view from Gerald's kitchen window. It was not just his wall, but stretched the length of the row of houses, divided by clipped hedges and fences. There was also a narrow footpath that ran to the side, between the houses and the wall, sharing the wall with the general public.

Twenty years ago the wall had not seen much action, occasionally things were written on it – *DEBORAH LOVES NIGEL FOREVER IDST – TOTTENHAM ARE GREAT.* But these had been in harmless biro or felt-tip – easily got rid of. Every year, around springtime, one of his neighbours would rally together the residents to dab paint over the scribbled entreaties and declarations of a stumbling walk home. And then someone had discovered 'the spray can'.

Numbers 38-42 Ashcroft Row looked out of their kitchen windows one morning to see their first tag, pink and gleaming, unskilfully combining the letters 'R E G' into a single-symbol squiggle in the April sunshine.

"What can we do?" asked Peggy, (number 38, blue rinse, yellow housecoat, fake pearls, duster).

"How are we going to get it off?" asked Barbara, (number 40, beige cardigan, pink-rimmed glasses, white hair)

"Shall we call the police?" trilled Peggy, wringing her hands fearfully.

A second tag appeared the next night, this time in front of numbers 44-48. And then 48-52. A sheet of photocopied paper was pushed by Gladys, (number 56, small, wiry, blue housecoat, tufty hair), through every letterbox:

Tackling the Graffiti Problem

As most of you must be aware by now, the wall behind our houses is rapidly becoming a target for vandals. Unfortunately there is nothing the police can do – but we can all make a concerted effort to be on the look out at all times, and help put a stop to this growing problem. I hope everyone takes this matter seriously.

Gerald had done his bit. He now sat in the kitchen to drink his morning tea, and had pulled his chair to face the window directly so he could watch the wall without appearing unnatural. Through thick-rimmed spectacles and recovering cataracts, the eyes of Ashcroft Row constantly scanned The Wall.

Through certain circles came the talk of this newly-found bare stretch of canvas. More signatures, graphics, cartoons, and mottos, arrived. Gerald found himself noticing two distinctive styles on his section that shone out and held more weight compared to the rest. He felt oddly privileged to have what he considered to be the best part of the wall, even though it was vandalism, it was *talented* vandalism.

One was a woman. She was not looking directly out but had her eyes downcast. To Gerald she looked sorrowful, but he liked looking at her, liked the peaceful face. The other artist dealt mainly in words and seemed to think seriously about what he said. His writing was strange, *poetic* even. *I whisper inside until I fly* – Gerald liked that.

Gone were the days of Deborah loving Nigel. These kids thought about it – and meant it. They actually went out at night and sprayed their writings on a wall for the world to see. Notebooks and diaries seemingly not enough.

The following spring, the row decided to take action. Another piece of photocopied paper was pushed thorough letterboxes requiring a whole weekend being dedicated to the Clean Up of The Wall. If the police couldn't do anything, they would have to take the matter into their own hands.

"Think of what it could lead to," said Shirley, (number 58, arms folded across her bolstered red cardigan, pince-nez on a chain). "A graffitied wall can send out all kinds of messages – that we encourage this sort of thing. It will attract all the wrong kind of people … and think of number 42 who are trying to sell!"

The weekend came and Gerald approached his wall with a sense of reluctance. Although the rest of the wall deserved a scrubbing over, his own 'paintings' seemed too good to cover up. He paused in front of them, scourer and bucket in hand, studying the woman's downcast eyes.

"Come on, Gerald!" shrilled out Barbara. "We'll show them who's boss!"

By Sunday afternoon, the wall had been restored to its former blankness. To Gerald, it looked oddly bare, like a house with the Christmas decorations taken down.

Two nights after The Great Clean Up, Ashcroft Row caught themselves a vandal. Spray-can in hand, he had been jumped upon by Gladys in curlers. She had rushed outside armed with a hairbrush. Her husband Bernhard, an ex-security guard, lumbered out after her and had him under his knee in minutes.

In certain circles word got around that a tagger had been arrested – had blurted certain names … pictures were left unfinished around the city, signatures without their signers. It was a shame, some said, sadly shaking their heads. Now the amateurs were wiped off, The Wall was now ripe for serious pieces … quality works. *Ah* they said – *that huge blank space* …

Ashcroft Row Wall received no unsolicited writing for the next two months. The inhabitants looked out of their kitchen windows at the plain magnolia painted bricks with satisfaction. Gerald still had his morning tea in the kitchen, gazing at the spot where the woman's face had been, remembering her eyelashes. It was on one of these mornings that he noticed a line of paint on the very bottom of his piece of wall. He squinted out of his window and saw that it was writing, but indecipherably small.

Gerald crossed the lawn in front of his house, glancing over his shoulder to see if Barbara was watching from her living room post – but all was clear.

He squatted down to peer at the small neat writing – undoubtedly sprayed on, Gerald wondered how they kept the letters readable while at the same time having a distinctive a style to them.

HELLO, IT'S ME. IS THAT YOU?

And that's all it said. He stood up, considering the sentence. He was sure it wasn't meant for him, but it was for someone. He patted the grass to cover the words up and walked away.

Three days later, the message had been answered. Gerald spotted it at once, on his way into town. It was at the same level as the first, but on the other side.

YES ARE YOU READING?

Gerald turned his head quickly away and smiled to himself. Another message appeared:

AND WRITING ... TO YOU

The next few came in consecutive days

FOR ME?

A NOTE JUST TO SAY ... I'VE MISSED YOU

A conversation was taking place between two people who were strangers to Gerald, but he felt honoured that they had specifically chosen his piece of wall to write on. It was like an affair of some sort, as if the words couldn't be spoken, but written, silently, and in secret – if you could call his wall 'secret'.

Gerald was pondering this when the doorbell rang. On his doorstep stood Gladys, Barbara and Peggy, wearing three identical forced smiles. He knew why they were there the moment he saw them.

"Gerald – " began Gladys sweetly, "we were all quite concerned as to whether you'd be at home or not."

"Why's that?" asked Gerald innocently.

"Well ... we were all sure you'd been away for the past few days."

"No," shrugged Gerald, "I've been here all the time."

"I see ... Well, in that case why have you not done anything about the vandalism on your wall?"

"What vandalism?"

"Now, Gerald," smiled Gladys, as she would with a child, "surely you must have seen the new stuff that's appeared there ... I do hope you intend to take responsibility for your section."

"But it's only on my piece," answered Gerald defiantly. He had not even considered painting over it – he had been too eager to see what was going to be written next.

"Yes, but it only takes one to start it off again … Now, are you going to take it off?"

"Have you read what's on there?" he suddenly asked.

"No I haven't, Gerald," snapped Gladys impatiently. "Does it matter? It's making a mess on our wall. Now, are you going to take it off?"

Gerald made a quick decision on the spot. "No, I'm not," he said bluntly. "I like the writing, it's poetic and artistic – something you lot wouldn't know about." And before they could begin again, he added, "It's not a mess. It's a message board, and it's got to stay there for them."

"For *whom*, Gerald?" squawked Gladys. "Exactly whose wall is it?"

"It's more mine than yours," replied Gerald simply. "And the writing stays." And with that he shut the door swiftly. That afternoon he painted over the words with thick clear varnish – ensuring a watertight seal impenetrable to any dabs of magnolia.

I WAS WRITING TO ASK …

Said the next message.

I THINK I LEFT
A PART OF MYSELF WITH YOU.
COULD I STOP BY AND PICK IT UP?

The recipient was silent for a few days and then suddenly surfaced, sounding, Gerald thought, urgent and somehow despairing.

THERE ARE TIMES WHEN I CANNOT BEAR
TO WRITE YOUR NAME,
BUT NOW YOUR IMAGE IS EVERYWHERE,
IN THE WALLS AND PAVEMENT

CITIES, HOUSES, PEOPLE,
GET STUCK IN YOUR TEETH,
LIKE FUDGE, LIKE SUGAR,
WEDGED IN, SHATTERING THE ENAMEL
– I CANNOT THINK OF YOU

Gerald's lip trembled when he read that, one grey dismal day. The writing had seemed so sad recently, it sucked Gerald back to one similar grey day, when he had said goodbye to Alice. He would never have dared to write to her with these words, but looking at them now, they described what he had been feeling perfectly.

The next night the wall read: *STOP*

'Stop?' thought Gerald in a panic. 'No, please, don't stop.'

No writing appeared for the next two weeks. He worried for these two strangers who had unknowingly drawn him into their secret.

Then, just as Gerald was adjusting back into his usual routine of having his morning tea in the living room, he noticed a familiar line of blue paint that had not been there before: –

WE CAN'T DO SUCH VIOLENT ACTS TO OUR HEARTS AND MINDS – NOT YET. NOW. P.M.

Gerald's heart gave a jolt, he knew what the writer was implying, 'They can't say goodbye …'

He fell into a light doze and awoke half an hour later, jerking his head towards the window. Another line had been added:

THIS LINE TELLS OF MY PROMISE

He cursed himself for falling asleep. Whoever the red spray can belonged had come that very afternoon and taken a huge risk by graffiti-ing in daylight. It was a response, and a dedicated one at that.

That evening he took up his post at the window, eyes constantly glued to the darkened wall. For five hours he waited. At around 2 am Gerald was startled by footsteps on the path, he peered into the darkness. A small figure appeared, dressed in black. It was a girl. When she glanced behind her, Gerald caught sight of her face and was astonished at how young she looked, 15 maybe 16, with a small fresh face and dark flashing eyes.

'Surely it can't be her,' thought Gerald. The mature words did not seem to fit with this slight girl. There was a coarse rattle and the thin hiss of a spray can, and then came Gerald's second shock of the early morning:

WHATEVER YOU DO, DON'T WALK AWAY

The girl was writing in blue. Gerald had always supposed the blue message to be from a man. Gerald never imagined them to be female, and he thought again of Alice: did she ever think or feel so passionately?

The girl had finished her message, glancing up and down the road. Gerald watched her with a growing sadness, now knowing who she was waiting for, standing there, risking more by each second.

Minutes passed. The girl took one last long look in both directions and then turned to face the wall, her shoulders heaved a reluctant sigh as she lowered her head and walked away.

Gerald lent back sadly in his chair. He felt finality in what he had just witnessed. This was to be the last test of them both, and The Other had just failed the girl. A new sound shook him. Heavier footsteps on the tarmac. Another small figure, taller than the girl, and dressed identically, carrying a rucksack. A Boy. Gerald watched him with pity, as he read the new message.

Whatever you do don't walk away. But She had walked away.

The boy stood for a long moment. Deciding. Then he reached in his bag. Gerald thought quickly and took action. Slipping from his seat, he hurried to unlock his back door. Tiptoeing towards the boy, The Vandal, The Other Author, he touched his arm gently and the boy whipped around. Gerald immediately put a finger to his lips, his *shush* urging the boy to trust him. Gerald looked down to see that the boy was holding a stencil.

IF YOU HAVE TO READ THIS,
REMEMBER ME IN SMILES

Still in silence, Gerald frantically pointed to the last message written by the girl. The boy saw that This Old Man knew all about their story, that probably *he had been the one* who had allowed their writing to continue. The boy shrugged, gesturing around him to indicate that she was not there. His face was set in anger and dejection as he raised the regretful sentence to The Wall and set his spray can ready. Gerald grabbed it and as he and the boy silently struggled, Gerald made a final thrust for the can and aimed it at the wall, As he sprayed the writing came out straggled and uneven, but readable:

sHe HaS Not GONe – WAIT

Gerald did not know this for sure – he had put his neck on the line by writing this, but he felt certain that the girl had not left entirely. The boy looked to the sentence, and then back to Gerald who nodded,

"Gerald!" came a shout. "What on earth are you doing?"

A flashlight shone in their faces and behind it. Gerald could make out the shape of Barbara (curlers and dressing gown) standing on her lawn open-mouthed. The boy bolted, leaving Gerald rooted to the spot, spray can in hand, unable to speak. He suddenly felt a rough arm around his neck and a knee dug in to make his own legs buckle.

"It's all right, Barbara! I've got him!" came Bernhard's rough breath in Gerald's face.

As he fell to the path Gerald's eyes followed the boy's retreating figure. As he reached the end of the row another shape stepped out of the shadows, revealing itself in the yellow pool of street light. Gerald could just make out the two shapes moulding into one, separating again and quickly fading into the enveloping night.

He smiled.

Anne Ryland

Four Cousins over Dessert

We're together as women for the first time
sitting stiffly as queens,
each from a different branch of the tree.

Dessert is served on glass platters.
Four portions: a cream slice,
an almond tart, a rhubarb crumble.
And one stone, the shape of a flattened egg.

I don't want the stone – why do I take it?
The others are silenced by soft spoonfuls,
the tender filling of their bellies.

Yet my palm welcomes such coolness,
unplumbed hardness. I'm just marvelling
at the swirl of its grey sorbet sea,
the marshmallow pink islands,
the sparks of quartz

when my youngest cousin says: "You're so pale.
Have you ever thought of surrogacy?"

I slip the stone into my mouth,
roll it round and round – it may rainbow
colours like a gobstopper
or it might be a witch's pill that lasts for ever.

I smile at the cousins
but it's my rock face smile, bloodless.
This sandstone on my tongue
is a word I still can't pronounce

and never will.
I'll have to swallow it in one gulp.

Never so much as Larva

This miniature raincoat in Stop! red,
black spots on cuffs and collar,
the giant ladybird pocket –
I see her running through puddles,
mud-spatter on her bare legs;

I hear her shapeless coat squeak
with every jump and swoop.
Now she's huddled on the doorstep,
hair frizzed by the drizzle,
straining to steady her hand
as she paints dot after dot
onto red wellington boots.
Her brilliance from such distance
stuns me. And as I reach out
my finger to touch this happy coat
on its peg, I almost laugh but
it still makes no sense that I miss
my daughter, who was never
so much as larva or egg within me.
That all I can do at this moment
is bolt home and try to write her alive.

Rebekah

"Two nations are in your womb." (Genesis)

Already they were jostling within her –
one was a country of forest and moss,

bare feet pounding earth, slither of pelt.
Everything was red-brown and sudden.

The other was open terrain, slippery
blue-grey. Rock-ripples, water closing

over. No footprints left behind.
She composed her own map for each land.

Even the rain fell differently – it spattered
on trees or gashed against cliffs.

Through months of listening she learned
that the two nations shared a language

yet the same word was a leaf
on one side, a pebble on the other.

She sensed a father-son and a mother-son.
How would she hold them together?

Could both be home or would one always
be in exile? She rested her palms

on their softness, their bones.
Twenty years of emptiness, and waiting –

all the love she'd stored would never
be enough to stave off a war.

The Ruin Withholds its Secrets

Its raggedness disrupts the skyline –
my eye stumbles over juts and drops.

    This is no sanctuary.
    But there is so much room in a ruin,
        to tramp my way through a long hesitation.

A human in the ruins is less
than the whistle of a curlew across mudflats
or a single thrift swaying on the cliff.

    Under the rainbow arch of the priory:
    the depth of redness impressed in sandstone.

I love the silences of a ruin's story,
the presence of murders and prayers.

    I draw closer to touch
    its scars and fractures –
    immerse myself in brokenness.

Those who live only in their bones and memories
crumble so slowly, never
to be restored.

    Where are the stairs that spiral
        beyond rooflessness?

When I wander over a ruin, a longing grows in my throat.

    It has borne the ice, the salt-gnaw and the wars;
    it knows the triumph of being more
    than left over.

Such quiet defiance in a ruin –
that it dares to be an outline.

Elise McKay

Bemused

A cool, clear night;
a night for throwing logs on the fire
and listening to their crackle.
A night when the smell of wood smoke
curls up into the sky
and I cannot tell whether I hear
the colour of smoke or see its smell.

My lips taste of long ago forests,
as, lulled by warmth
I drift into half sleep.
Senses merge
as a harlequin might pass a glittering ball
hand to hand till
impishly
he tosses it up into the sky.

There it falls apart; sight, smell,
colour, touch, scatter to earth,
jostle together.

A shifting log's enough
to startle my wandering muse.
The fire is dead and I am awake,
bewildered by the kaleidoscope
of this amazing, diverse world.

You Have to Laugh

One day the Gods, being disillusioned
with what they saw below
decided to waste no more effort
on their ungrateful works.
No more free gifts,
no more indulgencies.

Then they began to plan their Olympics,
but got no farther than the first hurdle
when the youngest God pleaded
"One more, just one more, please!"
for he liked humans to have fair play.

Being in a hurry to settle their teams
the Gods shrugged and said,
"Oh, well, one last gift – but
make it small and disposable."

The youngest God didn't have to think long.
He had the very thing
that would stir things up
and tossed down fun and laughter.

They fell lightly enough to earth
scattering haphazardly.
And some, the lucky ones,
lifted their heads and sniffed the air,
as something tickled their senses.

So laughter welled up,
and the world was flooded with mirth.
But the Gods were puzzled,
wondering what they'd missed –
poor things – they had no sense of humour.

On the Shelf

Only the Buddha is missing,
gazing at his navel,
but here is the wise owl,
small and bronzed,
and the old Greek carved in marble.

Here, too, is the household god
clutching his wooden staff
and the poet, pen poised,
staring into space.

Above them 'La Liseuse' reads on,
as she has done for years,
never lifting her head,
absorbed in her book.

I dust them carefully, put each back
exactly where they stood before.
The world moves on without them
and I, no wiser than before.

If only they could speak.
Wisdom, like poetry, needs to be shared.

Pickings

Merryn Glover

Take my hand, Sanu-*bhai*, and I'll teach you everything I know. Just like your big brother, now hey-na? I'm rising twelve, yeh, and I been working Kathmandu streets since I was a chut, so don't you be scared. No blubber-babu, eh? I'll look after you – just do's I say.

First thing: watch those dogs. They hate us even more an the people do. Don't ask me why. They want same rubbish as us, but too dumb to look round an see a pile of the crap on every corner. Plenty to go round, I say, but try telling that to a stinking *kukur*. Fact is, they're nasty. Snarl and snap at you. Sometimes big packs a them, too. So just keep your eyes down, *babu*, and keep walking. My Bua's got a big wire hook he shakes an, oh-yeah! that gets em hopping! But don't you try that, boy, you hear? You just a little *chut* and not up for that. An you listen to me, now – there's some mutts around here that've gone mad in the head an if they get you – *bhayo!* You're gone. Uncle Kumar got bit, and *aiya-aiya-aiya* was he a mess. Frothing at the mouth and howling – *ar-ar-aaaaar!* – and rollin is eyes and then two days later – dead as meat.

La, but don't look so scared. Here – make a sling-shot like mine and you'll be tough like me. See? Twig first, rubber from some *chappals* cross the middle and a good hard rock. I've got tip-top aim. They call me the king! Get dogs smack tween the eyes and birds right out a their trees. Now, hide here and I'll try Mrs Office Lady's fat *chaak*. Ready, steady … FIRE! Gotcha! Yeah! She is HOPPING mad! Not bad, eh *bhai*? Not bad at all.

But now, Sanu-*bhai*, to work. Grab your sack. Work over this heap and stuff in anything we can sell or use. You find something good don't you sneaky-sneaky snitch it for yourself! Always show my Ama or Bua first. They took you in, *babu*, cause god-only-knows where your folks took off to, so you toe the line! And you look sharp cause there's a lot a crap in these dumps now-days. Shitty nappies and women's bloody stuff. When your sack's full, take it down Teku camp and sort into piles for *kawadi* when he comes to buy. Two rupees a kilo for paper, three for plastic, five for cloth and eight for metal. Bua swears he cheats on the weighing, but *ke garne?* What can we do? Shit-all, that's what.

Now, those guys over there, *babu* – police. See the big sticks? Fact is, after the dogs, they're the next worse thing – and you can't even take pot shots at em. *Nai, nai*, they don't find find it funny at all. Got that, boy? *No Hitting Police!* Don't laugh, I tell you. You'd be dust before you could say, "O-ho sorry, thought you were a dog." But *they* can do whatever they damn like to us, so you watch out. You going over a rubbish dump and they come by? Just skoot off. *Chito- chito!* You don't make it? Then answer all their questions, but keep your eyes down and never say where the grown ups are, cause *They* get the big trouble. Not so bad if they keep paying up – you know, 20 percent *dhamki dini* to the police – but sometimes they not got it, and that's when the hassle starts.

Bua didn't pay up for a while and the police were getting nasty. Giving him *dhuka, dhuka*. Then there's a break-in – one of the fancy houses in Sanepa – next thing – who's in for questioning? You got it – Bua. Police use a big heavy stick to ask their questions, *hey-na?* Bua got it bad. Ama looked pretty bad too, when she got back from visiting him. We had to pay three thousand rupees to get him out. That don't fall outta rubbish heaps, eh Sanu-*bhai*, if you get me.

So, *babu*, this is tricky stuff, an you got to really listen up, *na?* Best time is when lots a *kweeros* get all crammed in takin photos of a festival or something. So stuck in their cameras you could peel the pants right off their *chaaks* an they wouldn't notice! Once I took this American guy's wallet and he turned round just as I was slippin it out of his pocket. I just did big smile, stuck out my other hand – "Chocolate? One rupee?" He so busy shooing me away, didn't even realise his wallet's gone! What a *gaddha!*

So, there I was this morning, *babu*. Get the picture: Durbar Square, nice an sunny, big noisy festival, temples and palaces all sides, the whole place crawling with *kweeros*. Perfect. My escape route is that alleyway there, and up ahead, my first kill. A blonde in batik shorts. *Kweeri* women are trash, *bhai*, showing their legs around. Ama says no dignity. *But* big camera and many, many gold chains. Very fine. Now I work extra careful. Watch first. Ahaa… she buy one Buddha so I see her *paisa* purse. *Arey!* What a fat wad! An there it goes, back in her pack. Couldn't be easier, Sanu-*bhai, hey-na?*

I slink up behind. She taking photos of the dancers … good, good. Shhhhh, I unzip backpack, hand inside, wallet, out – and run! Up that alley! Made it! No one saw me – clean as a knife. Not bad, eh, *bhai?* Not bad at all. I hunker down and count. One, two, three, four, five, six, seven, *eight* hundred rupees. I'm rolling, *babu*, I'm the king! Wahay! But I don't stop there. Oh, no, it's my lucky day, boy, hell lucky!

I go back for the real prize. Big fat *kweeri* wife with lots a bags and two cameras! Bet her *paisa's* in that pouch under her belly. *Aiya!* She's had more for her lunch than we ate all year! Right, bit more tricky this time, Sanu, so listen up.

Sneaky does it. Sweat drippin off her nose – what a fatso! – I can feel her wobbling from three feet away. Slowly get that zip. Wait for big moment in the dance show … NOW! Tight squeeze – fingers inside – grab – pull – *Shit!* She's felt it! She's looking down! Wallet's in my hand! Shove it in my pocket and stick out other hand – "Chocolate? One rupee?"

But what? She's smiling. Nudging her husband, pointing at my clothes and bare feet, shaking her head … reaching for her money pouch! I'm out of here.

I shoot across the square and behind a pillar. That's when I should a run home, Sanu-*bhai*, but too damn nosy. You learn from me, boy, learn well. You get a little luck – don't push it.

I watch her from my spot. Her puzzled face, scrabbling round in the money pouch, then she moans like a dog and grabs her man. Panic on his face an he puts his arm round her – *chha*! no shame at all. Brings her over to some temple steps, right below me. She goes through her pouch, shaking her head, fat tears spilling, spilling. Pulls out a piece a cloth and blows her nose into it and – get this, *bhai* – pushes it up her sleeve! Can you believe they keep their snot?

I check my loot – two-thousand rupees! Wahay, *babu*! I'm doing very fine, I am. Just one more hit an I'll have enough for Bua. But then a scream.

Who the hell was that? More screams and everybody is running. I don't believe it. The mad dog. I want to run too but people are pushing, shoving.

How'd that damn dog get here, anyway? Police should a shot it. But no sign a' them and the *kukur's* here, all right, slinking into the square, lips pulled back, dripping mouth. I'm stuck behind a young guy, red hair, saddhu-style. Cloth bag over his shoulder, inches away. Just a quick grab an I can dash for it.

But that dog. Just in front of us the fat *kweeri's* sitting there, frozen, holding her money pouch in both hands and staring at the dog. He's staring at her. Husband gets to his feet, pulls her up, starts edging along the steps. Dog's moving straight towards them, shoulders big and hunched, fur slashed. Tail's half chopped off and one back leg hangs like a loose twig, dragging in the dirt.

Dog like that killed Uncle Kumar. *Aiya-aiya-aiya* …

Me thinking, if I get this bag and run, that's enough for Bua and I'm gone. But that shit-crap dog is heading straight for the woman. I'm sweating. She and her man are trying to go backwards up the steps, but they're not making it, just grabbing each other, shifting their feet but not going anywhere. She's whimpering. I'm shaking all over. Shove my hand into my pocket. My slingshot and a rock. And her wallet. One rock. One more wallet and it's all over. *Bhayo!* It's so easy, so fast. Just one. Stop shaking. Do it, *chito, chito!* Do it now!

The dog jumps. S-mack! *Ar-ar-arrrr!*

Right between the eyes. He twists once, lands in a heap, screaming like a demon. Blood spurting, spurting on the dust. A lot a thrashing then it slows down. Final twitch and a jerk; he's still. Slingshot hangs in my hand.

Everybody starts running and yelling. Fat *kweeri* hanging onto her husband sobbing, quivering like fresh-cut meat. People charging everywhere, but I can't move my legs. Saddhu-hair and his cloth bag have gone.

I just stand there shaking, looking at that dead dog. Then – *big shit* – policeman coming my way. But, wait, that woman's with him, pointing at me. Hold up my slingshot. Yes, it was me, madam. I killed the dog, I saved your life. But she's not looking at my slingshot. Oh no. She's clutching her empty money pouch and pointing at my face. The policeman's pointing too. With a big stick.

Like I said, *bhai*, after the dogs, the police. It wasn't my lucky day.

Take my hand, Sanu. *Aiya, aiya!* Softly, softly! It's still hurting bad, but you learn from it, *sanu babu;* it's gonna teach you everythin it knows.

Robert Ritchie

From a Mouse

On being turned up in her (or his) nest with the plough, November 1785

Well you're wrong, Mister Burns –
you patronising anthropomorphising bastard
of a bastard-creating bard,
hypocritical lickspittler to the aristocracy.
Of moral mien you're less than squeaky clean,
you jumped-up upstart ploughperson
with your synthetic sympathy
and pathetic prosody:
damned mouse de-nesting fuddled furrower,
– there was no *panic* there
in what you cutely call,
in your couthie dumbed-down demotic,
my … *breastie.*

You presume to know I'm Miss, or Mistress, Mouse
and not, for not so sentimentalising,
a macho mouse,
a rude crude brute of a murine,
like you are
of a man.

My mouse-spouse and mousekins, abode unfixed,
pretext for your meretricious phrase,
my mouse house schemes *gang aft agley.*

You do not see me *cowrin'*, Mister Burns:
I rant and roar with rodent rage,
stack acrid execration on your pudding head,
and pray – if there's a power above us all,
untimely,
time's fatal scythe on you shall fall.

Deep Theology

God is like a shoal of herring
He has a squillion eyes
We are weighed on his scales
We are found wanting
God is gutted

Mr Mouse – Shona Dougall

Birds of the Coast

The Joy of Suffix (Fratercula Arctica)

Frateruculology: the study of puffins;
Fraterculocracy: rule by puffins;
Fraterculaphobia: fear of puffins;
Fraterculicide: killing puffins;
Fraterculomancy: divination by reading the entrails of puffins;
Fraterculophagy: eating puffins;
Fraterculaphilia: the love, that dare not speak its name,
of brightly-beaked burrow-breeding birds.

Love Song of the Herring Gull (Larus Argentatus)

seagurl
preened-clean queen j'adore your goldie eyes
head-neck-breast snow-owliness so
peckable mandibles oh gosh
my gull gal
I your gull guy, won't you
duskwinged bonnie
come canoodle, come
bill, be bestmate birds
feather-nest clutch-nestle
feed fluffbairns freshfetch fish
proudspy specklings fledge
falter flutter fly
– gullfriend, my colleen burd
my sea-love spousefowl
won't you

Calling Behaviour (Sula Bassana)

Often have I wondered
what a gannet calls a greedy gannet
– a glutting, guzzling, guttlering, gluttoning,
gullet-stuffing, birdhogging, wingpigging,
gut-jamming, gorging, gormandising,
belly god of a gannet –

and I think they might,
with a modicum of ironic detachment
characteristic of the species,
call it a Hirtan, or St Kildan,
after the ornithophagic propensities
of those respected island folk

– who snared and wrung and plucked
and roasted and ate their flesh;
and hung and split and dried their carcasses;
and boiled their skin for fat to sauce their porridge;
and snatched their eggs and drunk them raw –

and whom the gannets
were mighty glad to see evacuated
from that dubiously sainted isle
in The Year of Our Lord Nineteen Hundred and Thirty.

evil intent

im going to have an orgy with all
sorts of perversions i said to the man
from the tent hire shop incest and bondage
and beatings bestiality fustigation
flagellation origami rock n roll i
want something to hold it in ive got
the very thing he said windproof soundproof
rip proof canvas posts you can use if
you want and pegs im sure it will
suit your purpose its our new improved marquee
de sade he said

The Turn of the Weed

They call me Heracleum, for I am mighty;
I speak as the spokesplant of our race;
I am the voice of reasonable vegetation;
I am a weed to heed: I am the Hogweed Herald.

Transplanted and ported to vegetal vassalage,
exhibited as exotics, as floral freaks,
Caucasian curiosities, natural gargantuan sculptures
in the shrubberies and landscaped lakesides
of your floraphilic aristocracy,
you thought we could be rooted to your plots,
bound to beds, hemmed in borders:
like worm, like leopard, we turned,
we showed our spots, we leapt your walls,
fled your fences and ha-has,
scattered our seed to the wind and the water
and made our stands in haphazard havens,
congenerous colonies, enclaves of prodigious verdancy.

We have given you, in sacrificial tribute,
blowpipes and peashooters and telescopes
and periscopes and occasional didgeridoos;
we have given you spectacle and huge rhubarby leafage.
We have been a peaceful race,
our umbels have loomed without menace.

So would you let our species grow?
Under the aegis of maleficent sprayers
you have refused to grant us sanctuary,
though our haunts be ever so insalubrious;
you have hit us with your herbicide,
necrotising our chlorophylled cells,
watched as we wilted and drooped and dropped;
you have swiped and swatted in swathes
of fracture and rupture and laceration.

We have been withered but we have weathered your blitz;
we shall be meek weed no more,
demand our loam, our exile home, our rooting ground,
our lands to call our own, our *lebensraum*.
So give us your railway sides, your freshwater isles,
your graveyard swards, your fenland broads,
your urban patches, your niches and ditches,
your riverside marges, your roadside verges,
your woodland marches, your marshes and morasses,
your uncultivated wedges and shelter of hedges
your wasteland, your landfill, your farmfield edges.

And if you do not listen, we will bristle
and blister your children, scarify with fell stigmata;
we will crack your tarmac, broach your tracks,
our purple spotted stalks advance in rampant ranks;
juggernaut cartwheels of whited inflorescence
harass your habitations.
We will appal by our spread and sprawl
and wreak a terrible vegetable vengeance.

We are the literal Triffids, unbound by book;
we are the hollow stem, leaning together;
we are umbelliferous, we are umbrageous,
we are megafoliate, the fecund seminators,
behemoths of herbage exuberant with the intoxination of ardent juice:
– We are the Hogweed.

The Tale of the Brother Who Speaks

Roger Simian

Each afternoon two brothers glided across the dust of ages, bearded icons in dark habits. Some unknown purpose propelled them onwards: through the days, the endless days; the weeks, the endless weeks; through the years, the endless years. The brothers were so much a part of this dust and these afternoons that we imagined they had squeezed up out of the land like healthy limbs of wood made brittle by the angry sun. The taller brother had guided his sightless sibling for so long that, to us, they had melded into one gnarled block.

Always we offered cooling drinks. Always the brother who speaks was bound to refuse. "I must refuse your cooling drinks," is what he told us.

"Then rest a while," we said. "Tell us of your woes."

And so each afternoon these pious travellers stopped a while under our plentiful trees, our daughters and sons kneeling hushed at their feet.

Always the smaller, sightless sibling listened while the brother who speaks uttered these words: "Our religion teaches me to guide my smaller brother in his hour of need. If I were a soldier for war-mongers rather than for the Ultimate Creator, I would carry my wounded, dying brother home across the battlefield. I know he would do the same for me."

Here the sightless sibling nodded.

The brother who speaks continued: "You see the worry on my face, friends? Life brings us worry. Life is struggle. In my life I struggle to maintain faith, unquestioning belief in what cannot be proven, faith in the face of brutal logic. But I tell the logicians this: my belief cannot be measured or dissected with their tools of science."

Always we offered cooling drinks. Always the brother who speaks was bound to refuse: "I must refuse your cooling drinks," is what he told us, as he and his sightless sibling glided off across the dust of ages.

So it had been through the days, the endless days; through the weeks, the endless weeks; through the years, the endless years, until one afternoon when the angry Sun was swollen in the sky. We remember that on that afternoon those familiar travellers, the pious brothers, stopped a while under our plentiful trees, our daughters and sons kneeling hushed at their feet. We offered cooling drinks. The brother who speaks refused our cooling drinks.

"I must refuse your cooling drinks," is what he told us.

"Then rest a while," we said. "Tell us of your woes."

The smaller, sightless sibling listened while the brother who speaks uttered these words: "I've been having dreams. A golden haired woman in blue robes has entered my thoughts. In her cupped hands she carries a bowl over-flowing with blushing fruits." Here the sightless sibling allowed the lids of his eyes to fall open, revealing two milky orbs. His body seemed to shudder under the weight of the wail which ushered from his twisted mouth.

The brother who speaks continued: "Who is she? Who is this golden haired woman with her plentiful fruits and robes of blue?"

"The Widow of the Graveyard!" cried the smallest of our kneeling sons.

Our kneeling daughters murmured amongst themselves. We begged them hush and the brother who speaks sighed a heavy sigh. "No, little one," he said.

The sightless sibling shook his head and from his parched lips came these words: "Child, do you not yet know that The Widow of the Graveyard is adorned in hair and robes as black as starless night? Do you not know that she carries a dead bat by its wing, not a bowl over-flowing with blushing fruits?"

We murmured amongst ourselves. Never before had we heard this sightless sibling speak. Never before had we seen him raise his eyelids.

Our kneeling daughters and sons begged us hush.

Again the brother who speaks spoke: "Who is this woman? Who is this blue robed woman who has entered my dreams? Is she sent by the Ultimate Creator or by a devil of the dust of ages?" We knew not the answer.

"Does she offer salvation or temptation?" We knew not the answer.

"Tell me! What does she want of me, this … this *woman*?"

"Your boots!" suggested the smallest of our kneeling sons.

We begged him hush.

"You see the worry on my face, friends? This woman brings me worry. What worries did I have before she entered my dreams? All I had to trouble my life were the weight of my smaller brother in his hour of need and the struggle to maintain faith, unquestioning belief in what cannot be proven, in the face of brutal logic. But now this woman, this *woman*!"

The brother who speaks threw himself to his knees under our plentiful trees and wept. We offered cooling drinks. "Will you accept our cooling drinks?" This is what we asked.

The brother who speaks looked to his sightless sibling. He looked to our plentiful trees, and to our daughters and sons kneeling hushed at his feet.

"By the Widow herself, yes! I will accept your cooling drinks," he told us.

Each afternoon one sightless brother of the cloth glides across the dust of ages. His feet have trodden this path for so long that any stranger to our region may assume he has the sharp eyes of the hungriest of desert carrion. Some unknown purpose propels him ever onwards: through the days, the endless days; the weeks, the endless weeks; through the years, the endless years.

Perhaps one day a woman will come to him, as once she came to me in my dreams, as she will come to any man who summons her. Will she wear the black robes of the Widow? Will she be a golden haired Bearer of Fruits? Only the days, the weeks and the years will tell. Whether she leads this sightless brother to cooling drinks or to the graveyard is of little concern to her, I am sure. Either way, she will have answered his call.

Ruth E Walker

Nights on Hudson Bay

January 6, 1772; York Factory
… but the decrees of Providence are unsearchable.
The Present State of Hudson's Bay – Edward R. Umfreville, 1790

Day 1

Larder provisions scarce:
we are dispatched
to hunt partridge.

Set off on a day
warm enough for me
to question our sense.

Young Thomson and Farrant
full of spirit, both
anticipate our first shot.

I tire of seal, game
all sinew; winter ills cling
like bloated ticks.

I long for Maureen's tea
the songs and drums
of our Orkney village.

We pitch at the iced shore
a fire warming the lean-to
gin a flame in our hearts.

The dogs circle as dogs do
nose to tail and tight
against the sleds;

yet in truth it remains
too warm and the stars
never more brilliant.

Day 2

We cross the ice
each dog pulling
fast and excited.

I almost lose Farrant's words
in the rush of wind, nearly
miss the catch in his voice.

Ross! I fear we are moving.

A teasing mistress
this frozen land has lured us
on a temporary bridge.

We halt the sleds
look back to watch
the shift of distant shore.

The smoke of water
between our frozen raft
and the rise of land.

Turn.
And turn again.
It is the same.

Wherever eyes cast
grey washes between
our drifting ice island and coast.

We are moving into the sea.

Farrant almost weeps
with Thomson slack-jawed
near to surrender, both.

Wait I say for the tide
surely the ebb and flow
will bring us back.

We ready our camp
and pass the time
speaking of home.

Day 5

Three days: yipping dogs
adrift on ice and
the ache of appetite.

The last of the cakes
gone, sugar meted out
to melt on eager tongues.

I am not sure which
will go first: the ice or
the too warm winter air.

The dogs know.

They return to old ways
gnaw on harness and dream
of escape and full bellies.

Overhead geese pass
too distant and swift
to ready the shot.

The birds know

Fly past once more
close enough to hear
the mockery in their call.

Day 6

Ebb and flow teases
madmen with the shore
we rush to make the leap.

Farrant slips into sea
spills body and soul
we rush to warm him.

The ice is breaking off
dogs, sleds and nearly all
drift away and leave us.

Day 7

In the night Farrant fades;
Thomson and I remain
eyes too dull to weep.

A seal rises from the sea
heaves onto the ice
and stares, waiting.

Thomson urges me to shoot
I cannot; the creature's eyes
look too familiar.

The seal knows.

The truth of January returns
a let in the wind; the cold
falls like frozen mist.

Thomson's hands now
so swollen and stiff my mitts
refuse his flesh.

Blue moonlight
kisses the horizon
as he breathes his last.

Day 8

This prison floe edges
then meets the shore
makes a bridge to home.

Landing so close
to the Factory
I breathe wood smoke.

Delirious, my mistake
is left for right—
travel from not toward.

Too late I grasp the error
attempt a bed; pray dark
gives way to light.

Day 9

So cold that hours consume
a mile; asleep I press
frozen steps forward.

My once-lost sled dog
strangely now companion
trails my pale shadow.

Together we find
the gates of York Factory
where fingers, toes let go.

My fellows gather
coin to ease my loss:
the Factor offers none.

I will leave behind
all wrenched from me
by this stark moor;

I turn my face
east to the sea, useless
to feel regret.

Seven Tears in the Sea

This island is as barren
as the heart that kens no love.

I shed my seven tears in the sea
washed they were
clear from my eyes
that longed for heat
on icy wind-born days.

I watched those salted drops
sail west from the pier
cresting swells
undertows and sudden currents
pressing on; reaching
Hudson Bay by spring.

They always take our boys
stout hearts and iron backs
sail them through
skwither and squall
on a Company promise
of savage lands ripe
with fur and pine.

A promise
as dry as a brin wind.

Ross sailed home last night
fewer toes
even fewer fingers.

There's no purse that can
fill the hand of a man
like that.

The cold there, he said
plitters about with a man
teases him into believing
so the rest stayed on
fools, thinking a grain of luck
will keep them safe.

Now my nights are dark
and ugsome, there's no star
in that sky worth seeing
if it can't be seen
with my love.

But mine's a Selkie dream
hoping he'd toss one skin
for another.

Waiting aside the pier
keeping watch
for my prodigal man
all those days
all those longing days
done now.

Sea Shanties

Sometimes they forget how to sail
and the mermaids tow them ashore
ears stuffed with shells, nets
anything they can lay
their webbed fingers on.

It's not the sailors
that need protection.

Water girls can't help being
lured from ocean beds
and pearl-stringing.

Those sailors knew all along
as they thrashed and cried
over sharks and salt water stings
they cannot swim for a reason.

Bingo!

Max Scratchmann

I come from a long line of gamblers. My uncle VeeJay was a self-made man who amassed a huge fortune and then lost it all betting on his own newly-bought race horses. My mother, too, was an addictive gambler but kept herself contained to small stakes. My Mum chain gambled, if there's such a thing. The pools, the lottery, newspaper bingo, one a day. You name it, if there was cash to be won and the stakes were low it was good for a fix.

But the real jewel in my family's crown was my Mum's sister, Violet. Aunty Violet was, like the rest of them, a gambling addict, and horses, dogs and footballers all strove to satisfy her vice, but there was one overall sacred cow on her altar, one holy grail to seek – Bingo!

If you could be such a thing as a connoisseur of bingo, Violet was it. She knew every game in every hall, a regular pinball wizard of the smoky Welsh valleys where she lived. Like my mother, she came from a generation of women who never learned to drive and was reliant on lifts and esoteric bus services to transport her to her heart's desires, my Uncle Ken not being a man easily winkled out of his armchair of an evening. My mother always said that Ken was a hypochondriac, and I didn't know him well enough to make my own judgement, but neither of them allowed little things like ill-health to interfere with their simple pleasures. Like smoking. And bingo.

I lost my bingo virginity at fifteen when my family drove from Dundee down to Wales one summer to visit Violet and Ken. I wasn't to know it, but it was the last time I would see either of them alive as Ken died suddenly a year later – no doubt clutching a placard saying 'Told You I Was Sick' – and Violet twenty years after that, our paths never having crossed again. But I digress. It was 1971 and my Dad had a new Austin 1100 and we took it on its first epic journey. Violet was ecstatic. Not because she had visitors but because she had visitors *with a car*. On top of which it was rumoured, but, of course, never, ever, stated, that my Dad and Ken didn't get on all that well, so there was no danger of him chickening out of bingo and staying home with his brother-in-law. Full house for Violet!

Night one and we headed for bingo in the village social club. I sat poised and ticked off my numbers as Violet instructed. I'd always thought it was a simple game but there seemed to be endless permutations and little women in headscarves all got into minute fits of glee when the caller announced things like 'four corners and bull' or snorted contemptuously when only offered a 'line'. Violet, revealing her secret identity of Two Pairs of Eyes Woman, kept track of her own card and mine simultaneously, keeping up a running commentary on the state of the game, local gossip about the caller and other players, and the percentage likelihood of it all being rigged. (I forgot to mention, *everyone* in my family is paranoid.)

When the evening was finally finished I was a bit like the girl in *The Waste Land* – you know, well now that's done I'm glad it's over, but, of course, it wasn't.

During the next week Violet took us on the Bingo Tour of Wales, to big towns and hamlets alike, hundreds of places with names that sounded like coughing up phlegm, all with the one uniting factor. They had bingo. We went to down-at-heel miner's institutes and tight-lipped women's fellowships, quasi-derelict cinemas and flashy social clubs, all of them offering Violet's brain-numbing addiction and all of them meticulously recorded in Violet's personal bingo guide book, every flaw in the system, every slight dating back to 1963, scrupulously catalogued.

I don't know how much money was spent that week. I do know it was quite a lot because my Dad actually had to go to the bank and my Dad never, ever, ran out of money. A careful man, he always arrived an hour early for appointments, carried umbrellas on sunny days and packed enough 'emergency cash' to end third world debt. And none of us won a thing.

So it's the last night and we're at some miner's social club somewhere and things are getting desperate. The evening starts off with an altercation at the door as Violet's not technically a member and turning up with three guests is considered a cheek. Not to be outdone, my aunt spins a quick tale of three Scottish relatives from the outback who are being sent back to a cultural vacuum tomorrow and need some decent entertainment before being condemned to a lifetime of Calvinist hell. In my fifteen-year-old world-weary way I think they'll never fall for it but, surprisingly, they do. We get in.

The evening goes much the same as all the others except for one thing. I actually win. As the numbers fall away under the fat nib of my extra thick felt pen, Violet, still in her secret identity, becomes very agitated, jumping up and down in her seat and finally screaming "House!" into my left ear. There's a not-too-pleasant rumble across the room and I hear words like "bloody visitors" while the card is checked. Yes, it's confirmed, I've won £14.00 – not a fortune but a lot of money in those days. A few people clap politely. One person boos – only in fun, of course – but mostly there's just a moody silence.

Violet mutters, "Keep the money deep in your pocket. They'll try to mug us when we leave!" And, for once, I don't think it's the family paranoia. My Dad snorts and says I should give him the winnings as he paid for my ticket and Violet gets a funny gleam in her eye at the prospect of a share out. Nothing doing. If I inherited one thing from my lot it's the ability to plan how to spend money and the guitar I'd calculated I would have saved up for by my eighteenth birthday has suddenly loomed into view. As Charlton Heston would later say, out of my cold dead hand …

Thus my bingo career ended, the official story being that I quit while I was ahead and not that it bored me shitless, but there is one codicil to add. More than thirty years later, on a dark and stormy night in a draughty village hall in the Orkney Isles, I played bingo once again.

If you've ever been to Orkney you'll know that it's not exactly the cultural centre of Western Europe, so when the local lifeboat charity puts on a fund-raiser most folk prise themselves out of their hood-backed chairs and put in an appearance. Thus we found ourselves at bingo. Now I have to say at this point that neither my mother or aunt would have attended this gig because it was only 'Prize Bingo', or, in other words, there was no cash up for grabs and therefore was kid's stuff, but they were both dead by this time and it was the least we could do in their memory.

So we showed up at the bustling hall door and were promptly relieved of a tenner each (which hurt) for our night's entertainment, which, in all fairness, included a famous Orkney 'supper' which, as usual, consisted of more food than a small famine-hit African state could consume in a month of Sundays. And we played bingo.

Age may have mellowed me but some things in life will never change. Men's love of football will always be a mystery to me, cricket will always be something that only the Southern English could enjoy, and bingo, well bingo will always bore me shitless. But when in Orkney …

So we play and history repeats itself. Half way through the night the numbers fall into place and I call "Bingo!" and am presented with a box of Christmas wrapping-paper, possibly the worst prize anyone could award me, other than, perhaps, a World Cup DVD. In our house we tend to leave our Christmas shopping till Christmas Eve and grab a wadge of whatever crappy paper's left at the eleventh hour, and it's usually so terrible we can't bear to use it again and just repeat the same performance the next year. As a result there's about ten-years-worth of half-used wrapping-paper packets lying in various drawers and cupboards, so being presented with yet another pack doesn't really thrill me.

Anyway, I forget the whole incident, throw the paper to the back of some little-used drawer and get on with my life, until almost a fortnight later when I run into a distant acquaintance. "Oh, saw you at the Sandwick bingo," she says, perfectly pleasantly. This is nothing unusual, on a small island community everyone knows everyone else's every move. "Oh, were you there?" I say, politely. "Did you win anything?"

There's a momentary silence and her eyes go steely and her voice hardens. "No," she intones flatly. "You won all the best stuff!"

Editor's Note: a novel by Max Scratchmann – *Chucking It All:* (How Downshifting to a Remote Scottish Island Did Absolutely Nothing to Improve My Quality of Life), was published in June 2009 by Nicholas Brealey Publishing, ISBN 978-1857885309.

Reviews

Three Doubles

Hamish Henderson: A Biography, vol. 1: The Making of a Poet (1919-1953), Timothy Neat, Polygon, 375pp, £25.00; *Old Men in Love*, Alasdair Gray, Bloomsbury, 311pp, £20.00; *Hugh MacDiarmid's Poetry and Politics of Place: Imagining a Scottish Republic*, Scott Lyle, Edinburgh University Press, 200pp, £45.00

One enduring trope in Scottish literature is the idea of the double as in Hogg's *Justified Sinner*, Stevenson's *Jekyell and Hyde*, and Scott's playing with myth and reality in *Waverley*. There are many theories as to why this idea haunts Scotland and its writers: Catholic pretenders to a united throne are harboured by a Calvinist nation, but also harbour dreams of independence; the nation whose capital was centre to the Enlightenment also ruthlessly suppressed its indigenous culture (the splendour of Edinburgh's New Town is also the imposition of foreign power). Many 18th and 19th century achievements depend on industrous, often expatriate Scots, but the nationalistic claim of these is complicated by Scotland's place in a 'British' Empire. 'Doubleness' may be the inevitable response of a nation which was an essential part of a great power while being undermined by that same power. These three books all explore this ambivalent history and dual identity.

We gain a sense of this ambivalence in Scott Lyle's discussion of the idea, articulated by MacDiarmid, that "no small people in the history of the world had so profoundly affected the whole of mankind as the Scots people had done" (p 13). Yet this triumphant claim is immediately associated with a sense of Scottish impotence and lack of identity.

> If Scotland is to go on shaping the world in the same impressive measure, the nation must bid farewell to the defeated Celticism of its past and find a different political idea, a tradition of radical Scottish Republicanism that combines the Enlightenment's universalism with a liberating refusal to hush the distinctly local voice. MacDiarmid predicts in 'Good-by Twilight' that

"The day is not far distant when the Scottish people/ Will enter into this heritage, and in doing so/ Enrich the heritage of all mankind again."The problem is, which heritage? Not the defeated Celticism, but as Lyle points out, "the self-declared universalism of the Enlightenment was grievously diluted in local terms to self-repression in North Britain" (p 6). Scotland's identity is deeply complicated because of its complicity in the very suppression of that identity.

Lyle's book traces the strategies, poetic and political, MacDiarmid adopted to address this complicity while he rejected élitist modernism's emphasis on the metropolis and maintained a commitment to the transformative power of high art. By emphasising the marginal places from which MacDiarmid chose to speak, Lyle argues that there is a consistency and a development to MacDiarmid's thought which has been overlooked.

The result is a clear, if nuanced, account of MacDiarmid's critique of a Scotland that had denied both the local and the universal, and of his dream for a Scotland that acknowledges both. Yet the case for consistency between critique and dream is not persuasive. That the international is only possible with the national helps understand how 'difference' has value and the "universal is the particular" (*In Memoriam James Joyce*) on a global stage, but does not address the conflicts within the nation. The poet, exiled on Whalsay, can say "This Scotland is not Scotland", ('Lament for the Great Music'), but he does not seem in fact to have resolved this problem himself.

If duality is the symptom of complicity in national suppression, what is the cure? One answer may be fragmentation and multiplicity, another to acknowledge the impossibility of authenticity, the idea that all nations and selves are to a degree synthetic constructs. After all, 'Hugh MacDiarmid', (and others) is the creation, the synthetic self, of C M Grieve, and Grieve offers a striking inversion: out of one, many. Hamish Henderson identified this phenomenon in Scottish writers as 'Alias MacAlias'. Lyle suggests this tendency allows Scottish authors to "circumvent an inherited national inferiority complex" and overcome "their Calvinist complicity in Scotland's self-repression" (p 31). It further suggests that the while poetry might create a nation, it also summons the poet into being. So, I am sceptical of literary biography: the subjects are professional fantasists, and yet the biographer promises to tell the truth about them. Perhaps the best he can do is tell how the poet created himself.

Timothy Neat's biography of Henderson does this by addressing his self-mythologising early on. Considering why Henderson did not speak of his years in a London orphanage he quotes Henderson's 1953 statement on historiography: "Everything opposed to the revolutionary convention is ruthlessly suppressed from the histories of revolutions by the same obscure forces that erase shame from private memories" (p 18-19). Neat goes on to suggest that "the idea that [Henderson] might be described as 'a London Barnardo's Boy' was not part of his self-image as a Scot."

The phrase 'self-image as a Scot' is significant because, while born in Scotland in 1919, Henderson left in 1928 when his mother began work in Somerset. He was not to return until 1945, after being educated at Dulwich College and Cambridge and gaining something of a "grand tour" (p 167) of Africa and Italy, where he served in WWII. From here on we are told that Henderson "knew his sacred duty to be: service of the Scottish people" (p 175). Given the undoubted importance of Henderson's service to Scottish cultural life and identity, his self-mythologizing of himself is of more than usual interest and Neat's book – based on friendship and generously-shared access to Henderson's notebooks – particularly valuable.

Henderson's service took many forms, and this volume covers it from his time as Army intelligence officer, translating the letters of the imprisoned Italian intellectual, Antonio Gramsci, a prominent figure in liberated Italy's Risorgimento, the establishment of the People's Festival, precursor of the modern fringe, to the establishment of the School of Scottish Studies at Edinburgh University.

It is perhaps for his work as a folklorist that Henderson will be best remembered, the recording and investigation of Scottish music and song, connecting past and present. The ideas and friendships, both international and local, which were crucial to this work, are presented with a detail and verve redolent of a conversation at Sandy Bells in which we hear the intriguing description of folklore as "a cultural continuum within race memory" (p 276) suggesting the future sequencing of the pibroch genre and an anxiety about the authenticity of the nation Henderson served. Indeed, the anxieties MacDiarmid confronted in his relationship with the Enlightenment are echoed as Henderson recognised that "Scotland, by addressing its own 'barbaric and pagan past', might similarly [to ancient Greece] 'civilise' itself and set in train new creative possibilities" (p277). Such remarks bring us to the questions of what, indeed, when, is the authentic Scotland, all the more troubling for being posed by a figure at once committed to preserving its past and constructing its present and future.

While the contradictions of these positions are not explored, Neat's book will be invaluable to the critic who takes up the challenge. Neat's long friendship with Henderson, including collaboration on many projects, and his access to notebooks, puts him in a position to make informed suggestions about his subject and relate the life to the reputation. Neat speculates that "it is possible that Henderson precipitated his expulsion from Italy [in 1950] – knowing well that he must return some time to Scotland, and that to return as a victim of political injustice would do his revolutionary reputation no harm" (p 252), giving insight into how Henderson constructed his reputation and allowed that to be constructed by others. Less helpful are speculations which are left unrelated to Henderson's work and reputation: "Hamish does not mention meeting Primo Levi when staying with the Ginsbergs but it is likely that he did" (p 247). Yet neither why any meeting is likely nor its significance is elucidated. In a section on the Italian film director Pier Paolo Passolini and Neo-Realist cinema vague associations are made, but never made concrete, and undermined by admissions that relationships are "unclear" (p 250).

Henderson once described the Scottish Republican Army, with which he was popularly associated, as "a shadow of a shade" (p 321). Neat's illumination of his subject's self-creation makes clear that the construction of Hamish Henderson was far more solid. But however well informed by the brilliance of friendship and research, Neat's speculations can sometimes so dazzle the reader that we lose sight of the delicate relation between life, work and reputation.

If we see Henderson as mythmaker seeking national authenticity while MacDiarmid, more real now than C M Grieve, confronts the myths of the Scottish nation without fully offering an alternative to those myths, Alasdair Gray doubles as 'himself'. In *Old Men in Love* he expands our expectations from the margins as editor of John Tunnock's posthumous papers. These present Tunnock's notes towards a novel set in Periclean Athens and the Trial of Socrates, Renaissance Florence, and a Victorian Christian cult. Tunnock's undated diary entries introduce and connect these "annoying purists but making the book more entertaining" (p 8). They do, as Tunnock is a better diarist than he is novelist, understandable given the disruption his sexual misadventures cause his writing schedule. He is not helped by the editor of *Chapman* and Angus Calder, who find sections of the novel lying round the office.

The reviewer finally meets his double in the comments of Sidney Workman. With so many interruptions, editors and commentaries, the result is, unsurprisingly, less than the sum of its enjoyable parts, yet, against Workman's advice, this reader remains enchanted by the work of Alasdair Gray. *Sam Wood*

Pamphleteer

William Hershaw's collection of tributes to various poets, *Makars: Poems in Scots* (Akros, 33 Lady Nairn Avenue, Kirkcaldy), includes, 'For Duncan', which, though written before Duncan Glen's death in September 2008, is an apt elegy for this 20th-century trailblazer for Scots and Scottish literature. For Hershaw, Glen *is* a makar – here alongside Robert Burns, Hugh MacDiarmind and Sydney Goodsir Smith, all similarly honoured. Hershaw cites Glen's encouragement as a publisher: when the "young, gey serious and blate" poet, who stood "in awe o skeilly, screivin men", sent verse to Glen he "got a letter back that said, 'stick in'". Hershaw's poems are best when in jovial, autobiographical mode. This serves as a timely, useful and enjoyable guide to those great men to whom Scottish literature owes so much.

Another fine Akros publication is Philip Pacey's *On Being Incarnate: Poems 1977-1989* – and Pacey also recollects Duncan Glen's talents and kindnesses, and his "way of nurturing poems into existence and into print". Indeed, missing Glen, when he moved away, was partly the cause of a long-standing poetic block. This work is as much a memorial to Pacey's life as a poet as a retrospective collection: he explains in his preface, "since [first] gathering these poems together in 1987 I wrote no more poems, except one at Christmas 1989". He goes on to confide that he "had nothing more to say, at least through the medium of poetry – certainly I lost faith in poetry as a medium of communication, and evidently I felt no further need for it as a tool for making sense of my everyday life (and for seeking a faith which I've accepted I must do without)".

This canny assessment of the agenda of many writers and readers of poetry, bleak as it may be, typifies the unflinching honesty and quest for faith and meaning, which drives Pacey's work. In 'Sesame Street', the search for the most famous fictional street in New York is likened to "those seekers after God for whom/ lack of success is no reason for giving up". Pacey, with typically adept and serious sidestep, pulls this big leap off, going on to muse on leaps of faith both televisual and metaphysical: "As if to believe is to substantiate/ another order of being".

But all is not so melancholicly absurd. Moments of real joy and beauty overflow in their efforts to approximate to the state of "being incarnate" ("as it might have been experienced by Jesus Christ" – for a professed unbeliever, Pacey is reliant on such inspiration). 'Abyss', one of several early poems dealing with birth, parenthood and creation, has his young son hurtling across the room, "at the last/ fast faith-full flinging of yourself/ head first into my lap". This secular collision of father and son brings its own transcendence, wonderful and familiar:

> a portion of God
> rocketing into me, detonates
> an explosion of Love
> I'm part of and nothing but.

Pacey is best when touching upon the divinity of everyday life, as here, or in a moving poem about his dying father, and in his 'last' poem – both here and, apparently, *ever* – 'Christmas Night, 1989'. This reviews the Romanian Revolution through the lens of the Christian story, powerfully fusing the sacred and the profane: the world watches "another birth of the right to create", a birth of "ecstasy, impassioned rest/ while History watches with bated breath". Pacey moves skilfully from the personal to the public – might this new direction help dislodge that pesky disillusioned-writer's block?

History, personal, public and very watchful, also plays a part in Tom Pow's spectacular *Transfusion: a poem of praise* (Shoestring Press, 19 Devonshire Avenue, Nottingham). Pow places history – and the process of private events and political wranglings becoming capital-H-'history' – at the centre of his work. Citing Auden's words, from 'Spain', "History to the defeated/ May say Alas but cannot help nor pardon", he captures the sense of pity and futility so often evoked by recent history and makes it the fundamental business of his long poem. The book itself is a joy, a rich montage of text, handwriting and image, with Hugh Bryden's powerful illustrations transforming the printed words into a wriggling, layered, living thing. The starkness of the woodcuts complement the poems, enlivening the work and bestowing moments of tranquility amidst the bloody maelstrom of memory.

Like Auden, Pow is concerned with the present's ambiguous relationship with the recent past, examining two of the 20th century's 'great men' – Muhammad Ali and Nelson Mandela – and how their narratives have interwoven with his own. It was the coincidence of the historic inauguration of Nelson Mandela with the 20th anniversary of Ali's the 'Rumble in the Jungle' with George Foreman and the birth of his daughter, that inspired this work – a collision of the public and private spheres irresistible to one so interested in the grey areas in-between.

As any good feminist knows, the personal is political, which historians so often forget, creating both a vacuum and a need which maybe only art is able to fulfil. Pow's work elegantly highlights how venturing where history often fears to tread can produce wonders of its own liminal making. The Ali-Foreman clash is central to the poem, both in theme and structure, and for the access it allows into the histories, personal and public, at work. Pow describes listening to the fight live, remembering the feverish sense of so much being at stake:

> for how can the fine things survive Foreman's
> sledgehammer fists? *His* is the way
>   of the world –
> we know it in the night – sure to triumph
> over Artistry, gentleness and Love.
> We see a dancer, we see Poetry,
> Elegance – the darting lead and he's gone]

In a boxing match becoming history, history becomes a boxing match – replete with gory violence, and a memory which remembers only the most recent champion.

I struggle to give this poem its full due in just a few paragraphs – every page seems to cross continents and decades of human experience. The Spanish Civil War plays a part, as do the works of Frida Kahlo and Diego Rivera, among others. This intertextuality gives the poem a familiar feel (Ali fights "beneath African skies" reminiscent of Paul Simon), perhaps reminding us of the many individual testimonies needed to tell any kind of significant history – especially when "History's as far from the Epic as ever it was".

Another non-epic version of history features in Alan D Jackson's *Robert Burns: Icon or Challenger?* (NGT Publishing, 1 Berry Street, Aberdeen). This is a jolly imagining of the Immortal Memory address as given by a drunken, disgruntled (soon to be ex-) advisor to a wealthy, London-based Scottish financier and New Labour crony. The work is full of righteous anger and indignation – chiefly along the lines that the stereotypical characters suggest. It starts off charmingly, cheekily, but the badinage soon gives way to academic tracts on how we have fallen away from the golden age of Burns, when poverty was still picturesque (hmm …). This needs to be performed and thus (hopefully) elevated from sermonising into entertainment.

One work which does exactly what it says on the tin in entertainment is Jim C. Wilson's *Paper Run* (Mariscat Press, 10 Bell Place, Edinburgh). Its cover features a cartoon vision of disaster – a paper boy chased by angels and demons – and, like a Scottish Adrian Mole, these poems focus on the agonies of the apparently (sometimes, actually) mundane. There are wonderful moments, though, for which Adrian Mole would have given his last tube of acne cream – as when the never-ending painting of a garage beam is likened to that of the Sistine Chapel:

Like Michelangelo, you say. I sand
and scrape at thirty years' decay; the dust
adorns my every bit, and forms a crust
upon my lips. All feeling leaves my hand.
I've had about as much as I can stand.

Keeping it simple and focusing on the familiar is a winning formula for Wilson, and this produces his best humour and melancholy.

Melancholia seems to be a self-announced ingredient of James Sinclair's *Gulf Stream Blues* (North Idea, www.northidea.co.uk). This rich mix of poems in Scots and English, provides wistfulness, beauty and real lyricism, alongside the advertised melancholia. 'Infatuation' is particularly memorable capturing the siren call of the sea; a watcher gazes out to the ocean,

that look disappearing
over the edge
dreaming of a lifetime
on the ocean. …
you would never be lonely
as long as the ocean
slept by your side.

His carefully-restrained language yields great rewards – yet some poems have wonderful linguistic indulgence. The cakes and tarts of 'The Baker's Delight' are tantalisingly tangible with their "hot butterscotch skin" and "warm pliant sponge" centres. Cream "oozes out/ in great fat dollops", sticky toffee pudding is "drizzled/ over in finger licking syrup", and, yes, "small tight buns" are caressed. This transformation of stodgy Gregg's fare into something so seductive may not appeal to all appetites, but left this cake-fiend with quite a sugar-rush.

Feathers and Lime (Caseroom Press, 13/ 14 Silver Street, Lincoln), translations of German poets (through language, not nationality) by Ken Cockburn, primarily appeals to the sense of touch rather than taste. Its gorgeously-tactile cover and design merits special mention for beauty and user-friendliness. It offers a slice of contemporary poetry unavailable to non-German speakers – with a real range of poets and subject-matter. We find Dylan singing in the *Deutschlandhalle* and Icarus falling as he always must, and there are post-war wastelands and creepy-crawlies, Calvino novels and Rousseau. Rudolf Bussmann's 'Nimm die Dinge' exhorts us to "Take the things/ Both the great and the small":

The dry leaves on the path, the carton
The tea gone cold, take the kiss
On your forehead, the whiff
Of peppermint and garlic.

Despite the slight whiff of sentimentality joining that of the garlic and mint, certain odd little details keep this poem and others of Bussmann's from leaving too sickly a taste. Tina Strohheker's 'And only the snow' is similar in its focus on such simple details as "an ironed sheet/ an iceberg/ a sheet of paper", using these to meditate on what Cixous calls "white ink". Perhaps it's in the nature of the anthology, but these poems are all fairly short and seem to be from the "lighter" end of their writers' spectrum.

Laurna Robertson's *Milne Graden Poems* (Selkirk Lapwing Press, Lower Kirklands, The Glebe, Selkirk) also revels in its lightness of being. Just as Robertson entreats her "shy little poem" to send its words "looping/ across my page", so the poems swirl and quiver into existence, bringing something of the landscape which is largely their subject. The constraints of this surface focus, allow the poems to shift and expand in many directions without over-reaching or losing impact. In 'Cairns', a night of whiskied storytelling begins with "weathered corries and white ribs/ of winter mountains", moving on to revelation: "as if a misery confessed/ were a sin eaten, I was free". This absolution ends with "an ambush of wet leaves,/ gathered on the corner of a gale", heavy weather bringing with it "the weight you'd carried".

Tough weather is often the subject of *Poems of Maine in the Nineteen Thirties and Forties: by one who lived through them*, aka Brenda Shaw (www.moonpiepress.com). This collection gives a series of family snapshots – some blurred, others fresh and vivid; together, they create a fascinating narrative greater than the sum of its parts would suggest. Read this for its anecdotes ("Aunt Edith had no eyebrows [...] Used to paint them on./ Trouble was,/ she couldn't do it with her glasses on"), its "Pet Geranium" – and also for its later, more complex, considerations of the nature of memory, with its recognition that "behind each act/ the shades of the past shape us all."

Anna Girling

Catalogue

Interesting time this. We seem to be getting ever-closer to an independent Scotland in Europe, but more remote from the important issue of what Europe thinks of us. Well, there *is* a lot here culturally for a start – there might be historical holes there ...Quite. Scottish history and the literature that intertwines with it has far to go before we can ululate too much. Does it make sense to expect to be judged *abroad* when much of our most important literature has been ignored *here* for centuries and vast areas of cultural endeavour remain unexplored? So, how publishing houses are doing, right here, now.

No-one could argue that Scotland's written history doesn't sorely under-represent what Scottish women have achieved. A kind of Calvinism (often sexist), jaunts under the imperial banner (usually military and nearly always sexist anyway), and then much writing about 'the distaff side' has made a sharply defined, tiny pigeon hole in which to shove over half of the Scottish population. Time then for a little more light! Edinburgh University Press has brought us a truly groundbreaking work: *The Biographical Dictionary of Scottish Women* (£26.99 pbk): 830 entries by 230 scholars listing some of the women who have championed and influenced Scotland. From the semi-mythological Scota, ancestor of the Scoti; the more substantiated Isobel, Countess of Fife – personally despised by Edward I; Jenny Geddes of St. Giles fame; to Kitty MacLeod, Gaelic singer and star of the Edinburgh university class that included Sorley MacLean and Norman MacCaig. And Queen Victoria (!).

It is an enormous undertaking. Entries cover luminaries of the arts, law, great campaigners and those who surmounted obstacles in less obvious devious ways. Its scope, its sheer authority, stemming from the excellent scholarship by many hands, is a worthy memorial to the late editor Sue Innes. Her co-editors are Elizabeth Ewan, Sîan Reynolds and Rose Pipes. It simply isn't possible to do justice to the major cultural achievement of this book in celebrating our resilient, inventive, indomitable and creative women.

So James Hogg (who's never had his just deserts) really ought to have been included! EUP triumphs here again with four volumes of Hogg's *oeuvre*. Three continue the run of beautiful research editions the EUP are running by Hogg: *The Forest Minstrel, Contributions to Annals and Gift-Books* and *The Collected Letters, vol 2 1820-1831* and *Vol 3 1832-350* EUP, (£55). The fourth, *A Queer Book*, edited by Peter Garside (£11.99) is a roguish collection of much of Hogg's best poetry. The most interesting is *The Collected Letters* which presents notes written to shepherds and lairds and everyone in between. The letters throw light on all aspects of his life, including the spell ('The Blackwood Years' in which Hogg wrote *The Confessions of a Justified Sinner*). Amazingly, Hogg has come to be appreciated for the rest of his contribution only over the last thirty years. EUP's championing of Hogg is immense and *The Letters* especially reflects the diversity of their effort. That these books are genuinely needed, is best shown in one letter which laments: "I am grown to have no confidence whatever in my own taste or discernment in what is to be well or ill taken by the world or individuals". Why, oh why, do we treat our 'stars' so badly! EUP's accompaniment of their research editions with paperbacks such as *A Queer Book* shows commitment and imagination in addition to their commitment to the systematic publication of important Scottish literary works. But general appreciation of Hogg's writing, and access to it, is something we have should be able to take for granted long before now.

EUP have also produced a glorious and definitive run of Walter Scott: *they do great literature notably well. Castle Dangerous* and *Count Robert of Paris* (both £55) are new additions to their Waverley novels series, impeccably and copiously edited by J H Alexander. No other Scottish publisher can rival this remarkable publishing record.

Iain McLean's *Adam Smith: Radical and Egalitarian* (EUP £17.99) argues that *The Wealth of Nations* and *The Theory of Moral Sentiments* are not actually contradictory. The book (foreword by the PM!) argues that Smith did not believe in people looking after only themselves in a brutal *laissez-faire* environment and that the current credit crunch should encourage people to explore his wisdom: Thatcher would have thought his economics way too radical if she'd understood them. This concise hardback takes pains to link Smith's views on economics with his views on civic responsibility working both ways. A liberal interpretation of conservative economics! Tories take note.

It's Not the Time You Have...': Notes and Memories of Music-making with Martyn Bennett (Grace Note) is a collection of moments from the tragically short life of a burgeoning musical genius. It is a powerful, lucid and delicately balanced text – a lovingly edited compilation of tributes and memories of this remarkable young man from family and friends, including Hamish Henderson and Cahal McConnel. Royalties donated to the Bethesda Hospice on Lewis.

Gael Turnbull's *There Are Words* (Shearsman £18.95) presents his collected poems, any one a potentially fruitful focus for meditation. Gael was an incurable optimist, with a gentle faith in the power of humanity, with 'art' in its service, to crawl towards better things. Opening at random, I light on 'Learning to Breathe': "I'm learning to breathe under water. Don't laugh." Ponder the ending: "perhaps the/ flood level hasn't risen so high in your part of the world, *as yet*." This book shows a man who absorbed the turbulent pains of the world, dissolved them in powerful quietude, and breathed out an overwhelming sense of peace and possibilty.

Marion Angus was once hallmarked as a "home-made Marion" by an eminent poet-critic, gaily dismissed along with Violet Jacob and Helen B Cruikshank as "one-song poetesses". In *The Singin Lass: Selected Works* Aimée Chalmers (Polygon £14.99). MacDiarmid and Hamish Henderson knew better, valuing their work as part of "the carrying stream" which trickled directly to the literary and cultural revolution of the Scottish renaissance of the 20s and being truly revolutionary in melding together song and poetry. She's not a major poet, but her dark, atmospheric poems have an eternal quality, and speak directly to the heart and the soul. Chalmers recognises that, as with male poets like William Soutar, the circumstances of the time need to be taken into account and its prejudices countermanded. She has the wisdom to look at the life as a whole, as lived, and not just the work by including criticism, comment, emotional letters to Mairi Campbell Ireland, and even an appendix list of poems *not* included – a mistressly stroke!

The biography *Auld Campaigner: A Life of Alexander Scott*, (Dunedin £35) by David Robb takes a long-overdue look at Scott's splendid corpus. It is a valuable account of his life and work as, for example, the first incumbent of the chair of Scottish literature in Glasgow. No doubt the onus of this affected his poetic output and fortunes, but his contribution was enormous, including his championship of William Soutar. He was a difficult man, often courting controversy, many feuds muddying the waters, but Robb makes it possible to be more objective about him.

Scotland in Europe (Rodopi €60), appraises Scotland's literary impact on continental Europe. Knowledge is about perspective – and to know more about Europe we need learn how it sees us and debates us. As one contributor, Ian Rankin, identifies, this book champions the invisible art of the translator. This book inspired *Bibliography of Scottish Literature in Translation*. There is still too little European academia in the field of Scottish Studies (with notable exceptions like the Universities of Mainz, Germersheim and Bologna) and work online is paltry. We still have an impact to make.

Also checking out Scottish literary history is Marco Fazzini's *Alba Literaria* (Amos Edizioni €25), using 48 essays contributed by Tom Hubbard, Alan Riach, R D S Jack and others. Its daunting 825 pages cover the entire gamut of Scottish literature, from the 12th century polymath Michael Scot to Don Paterson and *almost* everybody in between. Fazzini is the first overseas writer to attempt such an enterprise – this is significant in itself as an indicator of the rising recognition of Scottish literature abroad. There have been other non-UK stalwarts who have tirelessly worked this field: G Ross Roy (USA) and Valentina Poggi (Italy), both of whom contribute insightful essays, but there's no mention of the groundbreaking work by his compatriot Carla Sassi, who's not even mentioned. Could this be because she has tried to grasp the nettle of the political undertones of Scotland's writing, notably in her volume *Why Scottish Literature Matters*? She has also made it her business to investigate the work of authors such as Tom Scott and Sydney Goodsir Smith who are currently unfashionable (the former mentioned only as an anthologist – a shocking oversight). A similar concentration on the fashionable is evident in the chapters on today's poetry, drama and fiction, all of which focus on writers who have already made it internationally, ignoring others whose work is just as good if not better, but who haven't been reviewed in *The Guardian*. It doesn't do modern Scottish drama proper service to confine attention to plays put on at the Traverse! Otherwise, it's a very useful reference work, with many important new insights and perspectives.

On similar territory, it's good to see the reissue of Roderick Watson's *The Literature of Scotland* in a 2-volume expanded edition (Palgrave, £30), one wholly devoted to 20th century work. And volume 7 of *Scottish Cultural Review of Language and Literature, Scotland in Europe*, ed Tom Hubbard and R D S Jack (Rodopi, €60), examines the fate of Scottish literature on the continent, including a chapter by Robert Calder on another much-neglected figure, J F Hendry.

After all this cerebration, it is refreshing to come across a collection of Gaelic hymns, charms and prayer, in the *Carmina Gadelica*

(Floris £17.50). Floris have worked their charm on this bit of heritage, assembling the text sensibly, in sections; healing charms, waulking songs, augury etc. Clear layout and engaging annotations make this an appealing and potent emblem of our cultural past.

Kailyard and Scottish Literature (Rodopi €54) by Andrew Nash does exactly what it says on the cover. The term 'Kailyard' itself is emotive and heated spats have surrounded the kailyard literature of Barrie and co. Andrew Nash has made quite a contribution in formalising the debate and critically picking over both the work and its proper place. Derided by some, affectionately recalled by others; calls by some to completely ignore kailyard work show exactly why a proper critical assessment is needed.

Reviews in *Chapman* often surprise publishers – since they almost take pride in appearing some time after publication. But, launched only a few day ago (early October 09), is *A Companion to Scotsoun* by George Philp, (Scots Language Society, £5.00). It's a rare thing: an entrancingly readable catalogue of all the groundbreaking Scotsoun cassettes (now CDs) and publications created over 30 odd years) – a classic as a labour of love. There's a story behind each cassette which is told here – both a personal and cultural journey for George and his partner in crime, the apt-named Allan Ramsay. I love the one in the prologue of George walking the Ochil Hills with poet Henry Kinnaird and hearing the evocative notes of a peewit, down on the ground, to let her chicks know where she was. This sound left George itching to record it as "one of the sounds of Scotland". And it struck me that the notion of a mother bird so 'talking' to her chicks epitomises the entire Scotsoun enterprise: *telling us, Scottish chicks, where our mothers are!* We are enriched, hugely from hearing our (mostly male) mothers, and learning who and where they are. The catalogue pays fit tribute to the commitment, imagination and, yes, eccentricity of its trusty, talented and dedicated creators. ***Jonathan Washington***

Notes on Contributors

Gary Allen: born in Ballymena, Co Antrim. Five books of poetry, recently *Iscariot's Dream*, Agenda and *The Bone House*, Lagan Press, 2008 and a novel, *Gillin*, (2005) by Black Mountain.

Colin Donati: poet and musician, lives in Leith. SAC bursary to translate Dostoevsky's *Crime and Punishment* into Scots. Wrote theatre text for Benchtours *Yellow House* 2007; pamphlet *Ancient and Now*, due 2009, Red Squirrel Press.

Andrew C Ferguson lives Glenrothes with wife and daughter. Poetry pamphlet with Jane McKie (Knucker Press on www.knuckerpress.com.) When not time-wasting on Facebook, performs with spoken word collective Writers' Bloc.

Tamara Fulcher: winner The Poetry Society's Geoffrey Dearmer Prize, 2006. First collection, *The Recreation of Night*, Shearsman Books. Lives in Edinburgh and working on a first novel.

Graham Fulton: published extensively in both the UK and USA. Collections with Polygon and Rebel Inc, most recent collection *Ritual Soup and other liquids* from Mariscat Press.

Danny Gillan: keen musician in his youth; feels that many years spent seeking failure and misery in music world should have prepared him for life as an unsuccessful author – *see note end story.*

Merryn Glover: Australian citizen, now living in Cairngorms. Chose writing for its steady supply of toast. SAC New Writers' Bursary for stories set in Nepal, inc; 'Pickings' which won Jo Cowell Competition 2006. Writing first novel.

John Grace: born 1949, lived in Scotland since 1963. Studied Aberdeen University, professional musician for many years – albums, TV, theatre. Two novels, unpublished; two short stories published. Lives Mull, paints, writes songs

John Holmes: born Glasgow. Educated at Corpus Christi (Glasgow). Poet, playwright: nothing else. As Christopher Marlowe said, "What nourishes me destroys me". Such is my biography.

Svetlana Lavochkina: Ukrainian granny promised peevish headmaster her grand-daughter would love English and be a good pupil. She's tried to keep that promise. (*Puir lassie – the Ed*)

Eleanor Livingstone: publications – *A Sampler* (HappenStance); as editor *Skein of Geese* (Shed Press) and *Migraasje* (Stravaigers). Artistic Director StAnza International Poetry Festival.

Rob A Mackenzie: lives in Edinburgh. His pamphlet collection, *The Clown of Natural Sorrow*, was published by HappenStance Press in 2005. He blogs at http://robmack.blogspot.com.

Alistair Marshall: writes dogged doggerel mostly. Published *Psychopoetica, Understanding, Poetry Nottingham*. Is owned by a dog. Shares birthday with F Scott Fitzgerald.

Elise McKay: poet of long standing with 3 collections, recently *A Word or Two*, with Edinburgh City Council. Still trying to exorcise the poetic harlequin who keeps tossing up the ball!

David McVey: lecturer at Paisley Uni, also writes non-fiction, and is confidently expecting Kirkintilloch Rob Roy FC to win the Scottish Junior Cup this millennium. Or maybe the next.

Benjamin Morris: a native of Mississippi, educated at Duke, Edinburgh and Cambridge. The short form in poetry, though not in biography, continues to elude him.

Maureen Myant: always wanted to write but motto *mañana*. Glasgow Uni creative writing course convinced her tomorrow never comes. Now writes every day to make up for lost time.

Stephen Nelson: born Motherwell 1970. Singer, guitarist; writes poetry and prose (some published in magazines); busker, brother, wanderer. Heavily into silence & Christian contemplation.

Alan Riach: Prof. Scottish Literature, Glasgow Uni, ed. *Hugh MacDiarmid's Collected Works*. Four poetry books: *Clearances, First & Last Songs, An Open Return* and *This Folding Map*.

R J Ritchie: writing not of doom, gloom, tomb school but full of *jeux d'esprit* and *joi de vivre* leavened with paronomasia and polysyllabilism. Epitaph, "He had a felicity (sic) with words".

Cynthia Rogerson: enjoys old movies in bed in the afternoons with cinnamon toast and tea, (or amaretto). Was American, then lived in Scotland for 30 years. Ambivalent about most things, especially Christmas and family holidays.

Anne Ryland: lives Berwick-upon-Tweed. Runs writing workshops, resident poet at a home. *Autumnologist*, (Arrowhead Press) shortlisted Forward Prize, Best First Collection 2007.

Max Scratchmann: writer and illustrator for 30 years. Worked mostly in England but 'downshifted' to Orkney 1999. Now lives in Aberdeen; writing a book of his experiences in the Isles.

Roger Simian: has recorded John Peel sessions and travelled as far as Texas playing guitar in noisy bands with strange names. He rarely answers the 'phone but is usually kind to spiders.

Rob McClure Smith: lives in US; writes about Glasgow gangs (1930's, tenements, razors) and the Darien Expedition (1690's, jungles, swords). winner of Scotsman Orange Short Story Award.

Kenneth Stephen: an emerging voice in fiction. Short stories in *New Writing Dundee 2008* and on Laura Hird's web site. Once injured his thumb in a 'horrific' incident with a stickleback.

Kenneth Steven: full-time writer – poet, children's author and translator. *Selected Poems* recently from Peterloo. Enjoys walking in Perthshire and exploring the west coast.

Gerda Stevenson: actor/ director/ writer; dramatised *Heart of Midlothian* for Radio 4. Work in *Scotsman, Cencrastus, Eildon Tree, Parnassus*, Cleave anthology and *Invisible Particles*.

Gerry Stewart: has spent the last 3 years raising her two boys and is hoping to turn her attention back to her writing, between potty training and pre-school. Might start with something short.

Ruth E Walker: published Canada, UK and US; plays produced locally. Edits/ writes non-fiction for money; fiction/ poetry for love. Prefers writing to almost anything … except family, mostly.

Fritha Waters: lives, works and writes in Edinburgh. Survived Dartington College some years ago and has just finished a novella. Won a bottle of whisky at Traverse Debut Authors Festival 2006 and hopes to make writing a full time job.

Saint James Harris Wood: Gothic blues singer, on the road picked up a heroin smoking habit, went to prison and re-invented himself as a writer of the darkly absurd. darklyabsurd.com.